The Future Awaits Us

First Edition published 2024.
ISBN 979-8-9907569-5-3

Dedication

This journey began with my first book, "Poems of the Pandemic," which started as a way to stay sane during the sudden shift to a "stay at home" life on March 13th, 2020. It was my method of keeping my mind engaged during those inactive times. My second book, "Musings on a Life Well Lived," emerged as the pandemic persisted, but we were slowly adapting to a new normal.

Now, four years later, the pandemic has finally ended, and there is hope for a brighter future for all of us. I am thrilled to present my third collection of poetry, which looks ahead and completes my trilogy. As always, I aim to encourage, inspire, uplift, and motivate my readers, leaving you with a positive outlook and hope for the future, learning from our past while making the best of our present.

This book is dedicated to my three grandchildren, Levi, Nina, and Fredrich, who, along with other children around the world, will make our little blue planet a better place.

Levi, Nina, Fredrich, and all future creators, live your lives with two guiding philosophies I've cherished: "Together, we can make a difference" and "It is what it is, one step at a time, one day at a time." I also dedicate this book to all children and their families fighting the battle against cancer. Never give up hope!

A special thank you to my brother, Jonathon Fischer, without whom this book would not have been possible. His motivation was the catalyst for completing this project.

With heartfelt thanks and love to you and all my beloved readers!

Table of Contents

Section 1
The Future

The Future Awaits Us

The future awaits us.
We have come through
So much together.
Now, the time has come
To leave behind those years
Of isolation, of loneliness,
Of sadness, of depression

For there is nothing
We can do to change the past.
We have battled though,
We have broken down,
We have overcome
All the roadblocks
Life put in our way.
All the challenges we faced
Are now but a distant memory
As we move forward into the future.

Over the years,
We have lost so much and so many
Yet somehow
We have gained even more
As we live our lives
During our journeys around the sun.

Times of opportunity,
Times of challenge,
Times of success,
Times of failure,
Times of happiness,
Times of sadness,
Good times and bad times,
We faced them all.

With each new challenge or
      opportunity,
Becoming ever
More resilient, more adaptable,
More flexible, more effective,
More secure, more capable
As we moved along
The pathways of our lives.

We became stronger by facing
The difficulties and objections,
We have learned from
The pitfalls and confrontations
We have lived through
The defiance and demands.

Now together,
We stand at the precipice
Of the future.
Excited to move forward,
Leaving the past in the past.
Ready to face
Whatever lies ahead for us.
Knowing full well,
The future awaits us!

Taking Back Our Lives

There's something in the air!
Can you feel it?
Changes are coming
As our lives return to normal.

After such a long period of seclusion
People are starting to return
To some sense of normality
Escaping the cocoons of our isolation.

For far too long
We have been forced to hide away.
The pandemic and virus controlling
Every aspect of our lives.

Now, at last, we are fighting back
Winning the war
Against this hidden enemy.
Once again, gathering together
In the world outside.

Finally doing all those simple things
We have not been allowed to do.
Enjoying the summer sun outside on
    a patio
Sharing the stories of our lives.

Friends and families reuniting,
Happy to be together.
A nervous energy pervades gatherings
As we wonder if it really is over.

For the moment,
Relaxing in warm sunny afternoon
Allowing ourselves a sense of
    freedom
Taken away, lost for so many months.

We will move forward into the future,
As unknown and uncertain as it may
    be
Knowing we are stronger and more
    resilient
From the experience we have lived
    through.

We will sit together,
Enjoying each other's company
Laughing, loving, catching,
At long last, taking back our lives.

Life, Love and Laughter

We are all riding Life's roller-coaster
With it's random twists and turns.
One minute, steadily climbing
To the top of the mountain
And the next, plummeting
Into an unknown, dark abyss.

At times, travelling one way
At high, uncontrollable speeds
Then, without warning, changing
    directions
Never fully knowing or understanding
When that change will occur.

Much of the time,
We are off-balance and confused
Sometimes, unable to cope,
Wanting to get off the ride
Waiting for it to end
Willing it to just slow down.
Yet the ride always continues
    unabated,

There are two approaches in our lives
We can easily undertake
Allowing us to smooth out
All of the sudden transitions,
To regulate and control
The highs and the lows
We experience as we move forward.
Helping us to accept and enjoy
The sudden shifts, switches and
    swerves
We encounter along the way.

Throughout our lives,
The ability to love the
    unpredictability,
To laugh at the uncertainly
Will help us to appreciate
The unforeseeable and the
    unexpected.

Love and laughter
Will enhance our lives
Beyond anything
We can possibly imagine.
Love and laughter
Will help us confront, overcome and
    defeat
The pessimism, the cynicism and the
    negativity.
Love and laughter
Will help us to appreciate
The unplanned changes,
The unanticipated transitions,
The uncertain times
All of which will always be a part of
The roller-coaster ride of our lives.

Time

Time is fleeting.
Time stops for no one.
Time is of the essence
Time lost is never found again
Time is constant,
Always moving forward
Seconds, minutes, hours,
Weeks, months and years.
Time marches on.

When we were young
We believed we had
All the time in the world.
We believed we had
A unlimited supply.
But, once gone,
It is gone forever
We can never regain
What has been lost,
What has been squandered,
What has been misspent and
    misdirected.

In our childhood and youth,
Time meant little to us
But before we knew it
Time had passed by.
Now, in our sunset years
We know our time is limited.
We do not want to waste
What little we may have left.

Throughout our lives,
Time is a contradiction.
When we wanted it to move quickly,
It moved so very slowly,
Seeming to stand still.
Then, when we wanted it to pass
    slowly
It flashed by in an instant.

We need to use our time wisely,
Allowing it to take care of us,
To live our lives to the fullest.
Thinking, knowing, hoping,
It will be there
When we need it most.

The past is time gone by
Never to be recovered.
The present becomes the past
In a moment, in an instant.
The future is ours to mold.
It is the best hope we have
To use the time we have left
To make our lives better
Than they have ever been.

The Legacy of a Poet

My legacy will always be found
In the words I write.
My children and my grandchildren
My family and my friends
Will forever be able to
Read the lines to remember me
When I am no longer here.

For in my words,
Embedded deep within the poetry
They will clearly see
My recollections of the past,
My musings on living life today,
And my hope for the future.

One only has to read their words
To feel a poet's heart.
For a poet's soul is clearly written
On all of the pages.
I know the reason I write
Will be to leave a legacy behind me.

When I think of all the great poets
I have read throughout my life
I realize I have come to know each of
    them
Through their writing
And the words they left us.
This is their legacy to the world
As mine will be to those close to me.

So, I will continue to write
About the world I see around me.
My feelings will perpetually remain
    infused
On the pages of my poetry.
For there is so much in our lives
To inspire, to uplift and to motivate us
Watching the years pass by.

As we move into the future,
It is the legacy of a poet
I would like to leave behind
When I am not here
To speak the words
To those I love.

Let's Take the Time

Why do we always wait to pay tribute
To someone after they are gone?
Why do we hold back telling them
How much we care?
How important they are to us
Until it is too late?

There is no way of telling,
For we just don't know
When it could be the last time
We have the opportunity
To tell a loved one or a friend
How we feel about them.
None of us can predict
What the future may hold
When it may be too late.

Far too often we delay
Until a good moment has passed.
Always waiting
For a more opportune time.
But what if we wait
Just a little too long?

Should we not take the time
Each and every day
To let those around us
Know how we feel about them.
It takes so little
To let them know.
Yet we hold back
Often thinking, always believing
There is plenty of time
Left for us to do so.

Let's take the time
To give someone
We care about a hug.
Let's take the time
To let others know
How we feel about them.
Let's take the time
To show them we care.
Let's take the time
To spend time with them.

Let's take the time
To give a word,
A gesture of support.
Let's take the time
To lift up their spirit.
Let's take the time
To enrich their life.
Let's take the time
Before it is too late.

The Village

Written for an organization
That enables disabled individuals
To live a normal life in society

In order to live our lives to the fullest
We need to walk along
The path of life
Together, as one community.
Each of us achieving
A life of well-being and fulfillment,
Distinct and diverse for everyone.
Building a place to belong,
A place to call home.

We can create a life
Based on our abilities.
Enriching each other's lives
Accepting and appreciating
We are all different
Yet similar in so many ways.
Each of us simply trying to make
Every day a good day.
Sharing responsibilities as neighbours
    and friends,
Always looking out and caring for
    one another.

Allowing everyone to live
With dignity and independence,
Ready to uncover new opportunities,
Helping each other,
Empowering our strengths and
    positive energy
As we create and develop a happier,
More enriched life for all of us
Moving forward
Into a brighter future together
As one community, as one village
For this is Co-Habit!

On the Brink

As the world teeters
On the brink of yet another conflict
We watch, holding our collective
   breath,
Waiting, hoping, praying
For this frightening moment of pass
Without our leaders
Making any foolish moves.
Moves, once made,
Can not be reversed.
Have we learned nothing
From the mistakes of the past?

Our world has changed
So very much
During the past few years
As collectively world-wide,
We have battled the virus.
Together, struggling to pass through
Moving beyond the pandemic.

We need this to be a time
Of cooperation not division,
Of communication not concealment,
Of clarity not ambiguity
Of negotiation not silence.
Of synergy not sanctions

So many of us are forced
To simply watch, wonder and wait
As events far beyond our control
Unfold before us.
Events that could affect our world
For generations to come.
Events that could change
Everything that will be passed on
To our children and grandchildren.

So, the sake of all those
Who will follow long after we are
   gone,
The time has come
For us to demand of our leaders
The common sense to step back,
Put differences aside,
To openly and honestly
Communicate with one another

Before irreversible events occur
That will affect
Each and every one of us.
Before the mistakes of the past
Return, once again,
To haunt all of us and future
   generations.
Before the world
As we know it is changed forever.
So, we wait with a sense of
   trepidation
Standing on the brink.

Why Wait?

Why wait
When making the decisions
We know need to be made now?
Will tomorrow really
Be any different?
Is it really what
We have been waiting for?

Why wait?
Is it not better
To simplify our lives?
To move forward into the future
With a clear direction to follow?

Why wait
When we know we will not
Change our minds?
Is it really that difficult
To make the decisions
We know in our hearts
Must be made?

Why wait?
Why do so many of us
Resist change?
When change is what
We are looking for?
When change is what
We really need?

Why wait?
Is it not finally time
To escape the shackles
That have held us captive
For so long?
Is change not the freedom
We have been craving?

Why wait?
What is it
We are really afraid of?
Why are we confused
When the way forward
Is so very clear?
When we know
What must be done?

Why wait
When we are so confident?
Why do we constantly
Ask for the advice of others
When we know
The decision is ours
And ours alone to make?
Why wait?

Is it not time
To step forward
When we know
What we must do?
When there is
No other course of action
To be taken?
So I ask again…
Why wait?

Section 2
The Present

Out of the Today's Storms

So much sadness,
So much confusion,
So much depression
As we try to steer our lives
Through the stormy waters
Of these troubled times.

As our ships flounder and struggle
Against the unending waves of
     anxiety,
As we try to move forward
Through the storm,
Steering our lives into calmer waters.
We need to always
Be looking ahead to better days
Beyond the horizon.

Yet, when all we can see
Is the unending, grey fog
Of answered questions.
As we try to negotiate through
The mists of confusion,
Sometimes we lose our way
When we travel deep
Into a world of negativity.

It is at these times
When we most need
Our crew, our team,
Our support system
Of family and friends
To always stand by our side.

Guiding us beyond
The tempests of today
Into the calmer waters
Of the days that lie ahead
For each of us.

We need to stay with them
No matter how severe
The storm seems to be.
To trust them,
To look beyond
The immediate turmoil.

To lift ourselves out
Of the quagmire
That surrounds us today
Into a more peaceful tomorrow.

We need to never
Be afraid to ask for help.
For none of us can navigate
Through these days on our own.

We need to be aware,
To realize, to understand
Throughout our journey,
We are never alone.

With help of others,
We can and will move
Beyond the overwhelming
Tempests of today.
For they
Will always be there
To help guide us
Into a bright and happy future.

Today's Travel Maze

Lost, confused and dazed
Like so many others
Making their way
Through today's travel maze.
Watching the same confused
Look in their eyes
Knowing that others
Are seeing in mine.

Wandering, wondering
When the next cancellation
Will be thrown at us
Without any warning.
There are no longer
Any excuses given
We are simply told
" It's Covid! "

Which we fully comprehend
Because we are living
In the same world
As those who are
Making the changes.
But why does it all
Have to be so last minute
Adding to our complete confusion?

Are the days long gone
When we were warned
Well in advance
And we had time to adjust our plans?
Have our lives reached
The point where they will just
Spin totally out of control?

Even as the sands of travel
Continue to shift mercilessly beneath
    our feet.
We have no one
We can reach out and talk to
Only adding to the confusion.

While we try to understand,
We are hard pressed
To accept the fact
We can no longer travel simply
From one point to the next
Without the fear of constant
    interruption.

The world is becoming
More and more complicated
Each and every day,
Our daily struggles are difficult
    enough
Without making them
Even more confusing.

The frustration and the anger
Will continue to grow
And without having
Any control over our own fate
We will continue to wander
Lost, confused and dazed
Through today's travel maze.

Simple Escapes

Riding a bike
As the early spring morning mist
Still lingers in the air
And the damp dew
Glistens in the grass,
Covering the bushes and trees.

Walking with puppies
Through the park
As they sniff their way
Along the path
We have chosen to explore
Moving slowly through
The sultry wall of heat and humidity
On a sunny summer afternoon.

Sitting quietly watching an autumn
   storm
With dark grey clouds covering the
   sky
As streaks of lightning flash without
   warning
And the deafening thunder echoes
Shaking the ground below
The sheets of heavy rain
Bouncing off the pavement
Dripping from the branches of the
   trees
Creating a raging torrent of water
At the side of the road
Which quickly descends and
   disappears
Into the culverts along the way.

Feeling the cold winter night breeze
Rush by into the void of darkness
As one gazes up at the black sky
Long after the sun has set.
A million stars and planets
Appear high above us
Filling the heavenly body
With their twinkling glow.

In this complicated and confusing
   world
Of which we are a part, day after day,
These are a few of the simple escapes
We need to get away from
The turbulence, turmoil and trouble
Of the ever-changing times around us.

Those moments in time and in our
   lives
When we can leave behind
All the anxiety, the worry and the
   stress
Of the outside world
To relax, revive and rejuvenate
Our bodies, minds and souls.

A New Prejudice

A new prejudice in society,
Pervasive and invasive,
Is rearing it's ugly head.
One, just as dangerous
As all the other prejudices.
We have faced throughout history,

We have lived and died
With so many different ones
Based on religion, race and lifestyle.
Now, once again, we foolishly face
This new prejudice based
Simply on masks and vaccines.

Those who wear masks,
Who are fully vaccinated
Condemn without a second thought,
Anyone who is not.
Thinking of them, believing them to
   be
Selfish, foolish and uninformed.
Those who are anti-mask,
Unwilling to be vaccinated
See anyone who believes in them
As weak, afraid and misguided.

The divisiveness and divisions
Have become as dangerous
As any other prejudice
We have faced throughout history.
Mankind, once again,
Has found a way to fight against
Anyone who does not
Think and act exactly as they do.
Believing they are right and
All others are wrong.

The truth always lies
Somewhere in between.
Yet with this new prejudice

Solid, unforgiving battle lines
Have been drawn.
In reality, no one is completely right,
Everyone is somewhat wrong

The foe we should be fighting
Lies unseen, unheard, hidden deep,
Infiltrating all of society and our lives.
Yet we choose to continue
To condemn and fight each other.

Will mankind ever learn
From their past mistakes?
Will they ever focus on
The solution rather than the problem?
Will they ever overcome
The pervasive prejudices infecting our
   society?

I watch in wonder
As we tear each other apart
With this new prejudice
Rather than looking to the future.
Working together to move forward
Towards a life, finally free
Of this virus and pandemic.
One has invaded, taken over,
Controlled and changed our lives
For far too long.

The time has come
To focus on the real enemy
And fight the battle
That needs to be fought
To free ourselves and, once again,
Take control of our lives.
Returning them to a sense of
   normality,
Moving away from the prejudice and
   the pandemic.

Never Alone

Whatever personal battles
We may be fighting in life,
There are so many around us
Wanting, willing, waiting to help.
All we have to do is reach out
For we are never alone.

The world has become
So isolated, so divided, so
   challenging.
Everywhere we turn,
We can see the divisiveness,
We can feel the dissension,
We can hear the distress,
Yet in our hearts,
Realizing we are never alone.

For no matter what happens
The world will continue to fight it's
   battles
While we are struggling with ours.
We may feel others
Do not hear our cries for help
But they are always there
Despite the perception,
Understanding we are never alone.

During these times
Of confusion and turmoil,
We are often left to wonder
If anyone will be there
When we reach out to them.
Yet there is always
An inner peace we may feel
For we can always rest assured
Appreciating we are never alone.

All around us
A desolate shroud of isolation,
Of loneliness, of separation
Has descended upon the world
But we are resilient,
Together, we will fight,
No matter how disenchanted or
   disillusioned
We may become,
We will rise above, we will overcome
Knowing we are never alone.

No matter what obstacles
Are thrown at us as we live our lives
We need to know
Together, we can defy the odds,
Reaching out, helping each other
Through all the barriers,
Past all the roadblocks,
Conquering all the challenges
Recognizing we are never alone.

Just a Little More Gratitude

There are so many things in our lives
We take for granted.
Our lives are so much better
Than many others who share our
    planet.
We have more to be thankful for
Than we often appreciate.

It is time for all of us
To show just a little more gratitude
For all we have in our lives.
For all the simple things
We so often ignore
But enhance our lives
Each and every day.

All the good times
We have experienced.
All the bad times
We have learned from,
Always moving on
Becoming better as a result.
Growing from all the experiences
We have shared over the years.

We need to take time
For all those who have been friends
For so many years.
To give thanks for the people
Who share and enrich our lives

Those who lift us up,
When we are down
Who encourage us,
When we do not believe in ourselves
Who push us into action
When we are apathetic.
Who make us happy,
When we are sad
Who give us hope,
When we have doubt
Who love us
When we feel unloved.

For all the friends
Who are there by our side
Throughout our lives,
It is time for us to thank them
For making our lives better.
It is time for us
To help ours become a better world,
To make our lives even more fulfilled,
To show just a little more gratitude.

Returning to Normal?

Two years ago,
Our world to a standstill.
In only twenty-four short months,
So many things have changed in our
    lives.
Today, as we greet
The dawn of the new normal.
So much of what we have always
Taken for granted has disappeared
    forever.
We now live in an age of uncertainty,
One which we do not fully recognize.

One we are forced to accept.
One we will have to live with
For the rest of our lives.
So many things have been removed
Leaving us with so little of what
We have known throughout our lives.
Our freedom of choice has been
    withdrawn
By a hidden enemy that has taken
So many from us, leaving us
Filled with sadness, regret and
    remorse

Those who are left behind will
    continue
To fight to take our lives back.
Yet all of us will be forced to live
In this new world, this new normal.
Forced to exist with so many changes
We are not prepared to accept.
Forced to adapt to new ways
We are not willing to trust.
Forced to move forward with our
    lives
Even when we may do not choose
    how.

Depression and despondency,
Anger and animosity
Have taken over our lives
As we watch our world
Destroying and tearing itself apart.
For many, this new normal has
    become
Too bewildering and overwhelming.
Too much to bear as we remain
    hidden away
Pretending things have not changed
But knowing in our hearts, they have.

Always trying to recall and remember,
How life has always been.
Hoping that somehow, someday
Future generations will have
The common sense, the willpower,
The strength and the courage
To make the changes
That will need to be made
To return to a more normal way of
    life,
Similar to the one we have always
    known.

As we head back out into the world
Moving away from the isolation
Of the past two years,
There is a foreboding and ominous
    trepidation
Lingering in our lives, hanging over
    us.
A sense of unease and insecurity
Which could remain with us for years
    to come
As the enemy stays hidden,
Always lurking in the shadows
With another wave ready to strike.

However, together with hope we will venture forward.
With the expectation our lives will get better.
With the desire to make changes,
With the ambition to make our future brighter,
With the anticipation of a better tomorrow,
With the optimism of a return to normal,
With the excitement we have overcome the odds
With the enthusiasm we have defeated the enemy
With the dream of a stronger future
For all of us and the generations to follow.

At the Dance

Anticipation hangs in the air
Like a early morning mist.
The crowd slowly filters in
Adding a sense of excitement
To the quiet atmosphere.

The lights and sound
Have been checked and rechecked.
Everything is ready to go.
Excited chatter starts to fill the room
The noise increasing in direct proportion
To the size of the crowd.

The lights go down
And, so it begins!
Vocals, harmonies and music
Replace the silence
Like the Pied Piper
Leading people to the dance floor,
Quickly filling the cavernous space
With the flowing movement of dance.

The mellow music
Sings out to the crowd,
Well into their sunset years.
Their age and years seem to fall away
The aches and pains felt
Only a few hours ago
Seems to disappear
With the beat of the music.

The complaints of their age disappear
For tonight, there will be
No limping, no pain.
All are lost in the joy of the dance.
Suddenly, they are transformed,
Just enjoying the music and life.
Familiar songs from their past
Brings back memories of other dances
In a time long gone by.

The dance floor is filled,
Friends moving together in groups,
Laughing and singing along to
    familiar words.
The joys of a long lost youth
Fills the room.
Legs gyrating with arms raised
    gleefully in the air.
Age has no place in this room.

Lights flashing,
Memorizing the mind,
Taking everyone on a magical trip.
Pulsing to the beat of the music.
The years have been stripped away.
All senses are uplifted,
Carried on the wings of the melody.

The troubles of the world and life
Completed lost and forgotten
Replaced with the love of music and
    dance.
So many different styles of dance
Each interpreting the notes
There is no right or wrong,
Each doing their own thing in their
    own way.

Before long, all too soon,
The lights are turned back on.
It is time to return to the real world.
Everyone heads home
So much happier than
When they arrived a few hours ago.
Memories have been made
To be remembered for years to come.
Laughing, loving, living
At the dance.

A Better Day

A dark and dingy,
Gloomy and grey day
Surrounds me
Matching my pessimistic mood.

Clouds hanging low
Rain falling incessantly
Creating a sea of mud.

Pollen and dust
Lingering in the air
My head imploding
With unpleasant allergies.

Waiting impatiently
For the rain to end,
For the sun to return,
To brighten my mood and my day.

But it continues
Hour after endless hour.
My feelings deepen,
Falling with each droplet

From within me, hope is trying
To fight it's way to the surface
Only to be beaten down
By the morose feelings of the day.

The melancholy battle rages
As I sink deeper into the abyss.
Slowly ever so slowly,
The sky seems to brighten
Subtly lifting my mood just a little.

Then, a ray of light appears
As my puppies jump on me
Pawing and playing

Loving and licking,
So excited to welcome
Another day together.

The hope from deep within me
Bubbles brightly to the surface
As my day brightens, my mood
    changes
With renewed sense of serendipity.

For now, hope and love,
Overcoming all else,
Giving me the feeling
That today will be
A better day

I will break free
From any and all negative feelings
Holding me back.
As I realize,
The future is mine
To grasp, to mold, to change.

I know I can and will
Take it and do just that.
Breaking free
From the bonds
Of my dark depression.

With my puppies
Now sleeping by my side,
I understand the future will be
What I make it
As the storm passes
From without and from within.
For today will be
A better day.

On This Special Day

Today is just another day.
Or is it?
It is the day
I came into this life.
The day I began my journey
So many years ago.

Will I change the world
Or will I simply pass
Through it unnoticed?
Will I affect the lives
Of those around me?

Will I be like
A stone thrown in water
Sinking quickly to the bottom
Disappearing forever,
Virtually unnoticed.
Or like a pebble
Skipping across the surface
Creating a wave of change?

Will I be like millions around me
Simply walking through life in a
    trance
Or will I be the rare gem
Shining brightly,
Changing the lives of those millions?

Will I walk the same boring,
Worn-out path followed
By so many others before me
Or will I forge a new one
Untested, untried, untraveled?
Will life over the years
Become boring and mundane?
Or will each new day
Become an adventure of discovery?

Will those I met along the way
Remember me as someone
Who changed their lives?
Or will I be quickly forgotten
In the maze of life?
One of so many they met
And simply chose to forget?

After I am gone,
Will I live on
Fondly remembered
As someone who tried to change
The lives around me for the better?
Or will I fade quickly
From collective memory
As someone who quickly passed by,
Whose name just disappeared
Into the abyss of life?

Today,
On this special day
There are so many questions
That cannot be answered by me.
Questions to which
I can only affect the answers
By how I live
Day to day, year to year.

So, as I move forward
Starting another journey
Around the sun
I must walk my own path
Accepting each day
As a special gift.
Helping to make the lives
Of those around me happier
Than they would have been
Had I not been a part of them.

Through the times of my life,
Writing a new script,
Singing a new song,
Creating a new vision,
Always trying

To make a difference,
To change lives,
To make this world
A little better each day.

The Show Was Over!

It was absolutely surreal.
On stage, the sets were in place,
The props were ready to go,
We delivered our lines,
We sang our songs,
We told our story.

Then, without warning,
Interrupted by a woman's scream.
A man was down in the back of the
    theatre.
Suddenly, house lights went on!
The show stopped dead in it's tracks.

Concern on stage, confusion in the
    crowd
The audience sat in silence, wonder
    and disbelief.
So many questions without answers
The flurry of activity in the back row
    continued
As the actors gathered on stage
Unsure of what to do next.

Suddenly, as people called for help.
From the stage, we tried to calm the
    crowd.
Before long, the man was carried
    outside
But the show was over.
There was no desire, no impulse,
No inclination to continue that day.

Real life had interrupted and
    intervened,
Ending the story on stage.
There will be another show on
    another day
But not today.
There was an air of anxiety and
    disbelief
As the audience silently filtered out
    into the street.

The cast and crew cleared the stage
For today, there would be
No more lines to be delivered,
No more songs to be sung.
The show had ended without
    completion.

As the reality sank in
As real life took hold,
We slowly exited the theatre,
Shaken and confused
By what we had witnessed
We will be back another day
But, for today, the show was over.

A Good Day Every Day

It is easy to make
Today a good day for ourselves
But when we make it a good day
For those who need our help,
It becomes an even better one for us.

Working together,
We can make each day-
A good day.
For everyone deserves the freedom
To live without restrictions.

To be able to live our lives,
Each and every day,
The way we want to live.
Sometimes, others just need help
To make that happen.

Each of our days will be brighter
When we bring the sunshine
Into the lives of others
With the ability and liberty
To live on their own.

It takes only a little, working as one,
To help lift others into the sunlight.
It is our duty to assist
Where we can can,
To do what needs to be done.

In the end,
We will all live better lives
By helping others to live
    independently.
Making a good day-every day
For the community around us.

Off To See The World!

When we met
You were just a little boy.
So talented, so excited, so gifted
But just a little boy.

Over the years,
You've grown into a young man.
Even more talented,
Even more excited,
Even more gifted
Ready to face the world,
To explore all that life holds for you.

Your family and friends
Are so very proud of you.
We are so happy for you
Yet sad to see you go.

We all share
This strange emotional conflict
As we prepare to say "au revoir "
For it is not good-bye,
Simply "see you again" one day.

Life will not be the same
Without you.
Life will change
While you are gone.
But always remember
We are here for you.
Cheering you on from far away.

Then, one day in the future,
You will return to us
You will be changed in many ways,
You will come back to us,
A man of the world!

We will wait patiently,
As patiently as we can,
For your return.
There will be fears,
There will be tears
But they will be of happiness for you.

So, after
All the hugs, all the well-wishes,
All the tears, all the kisses,
You will leave us and go
Off to see the world!

Mutual Respect

Has mutual respect
Died forever in our world?
Differing opinions and beliefs
Are now mercilessly attacked
By those who do not share the same.

Compromise and meeting of minds,
Now long forgotten ways of life.
Is there no hope of reconciliation?
Are we committed to living a life
Of constant assault and retribution?

There has to be a better way.
Why do we follow leaders
Who lie, cheat and steal
To gain power
While so many live
In fear of repeating
The mistakes of the past?

Have we learned nothing
From our history?
For many of us,
The time to make change
Has passed by.

Our only hope lies
With future generations
To correct the discord
We have created.
To regain the respect
We have lost.
To reconcile
And regain the balance
We once enjoyed.

We must have
The hope and expectation
That those who follow us
Will make the changes
Required to reignite
The mutual respect
Now missing from our lives.

Section 3

The Past

Evoking Echoes

The sight
Of an apple tree
In full bloom in the spring
And bulging with ripened fruit in the
    summer.

The sound
Of a train's whistle
Blowing in the distance
Late at night.

Or the haunting cry of a loon
Echoing across the lake
As the sun rises.

The smell
Of wild lilac
Blossoming on a bush
By the side of the road
As I pass by.

The taste
Of melting butter on warm toast
At breakfast in the morning.

The touch
Of a mother's hand
Gently rubbing away,
Erasing from my mind
The hurt of another battle fought.

All of these trigger memories
Taking me back
To a simpler, more gentle
Time in my life.

A time
Free from the pressing problems
Challenging me today.

An age
When I did not have
To think ahead with trepidation,
Worried about what the future may
    bring.

The years
When spring changed into summer
Summer to autumn,
Autumn to winter
When winter passed into spring
Allowing me to simply enjoy
The changing of the seasons
Each bringing different
Sights, sounds and smells,
With their own contrasting freedoms
As I explored the world around me.

Something as pure and simple
As an apple tree,
A train's whistle,
A wild lilac bush,
Butter on toast,
A mother's gentle touch
Has the power to take me back.

Remembering, reliving my childhood,
With memories hidden deep
In the recesses of my mind.
Always waiting to emerge
To simplify the complications
Of my life.

Evoking the echoes of my past
Allowing me to escape
Even for a moment.
Before returning to reality of today,
Ready to confront and overcome
The challenges of my life.

Trying to Remember

As the years pass by,
As we grow older and more weary,
Our memories sometimes fade.
Obscuring our recollections,
Concealing our reminisces,
Disguising our reflections,

The images and echoes of our past
Always altered, forever changing.
Did those pictures we recall
From our early years really happen
Or are they simply
Deceptions of our imaginations?

There are so many events and
    experiences
That we believe happened
Or are they simply snapshots,
Conjured and changed,
Recreated and reworked within our
    minds
From so long ago?

Do our minds play games
With our own past?
Are we confusing
Fact with fiction?
Truth with fantasy?
Reality with confabulation?

Hidden deep within
The recesses of our memories.
Transitioning and transforming,
Modifying and mutating,
Revising and reconstructing
The many exploits
From when we were young.

With the passing of years
It becomes more difficult
To bring back, to recall,
To take an easy trip down memory
    lane.
Yet from deep within each of us
From time to time when least
    expected,
Snippets of our past,
Real or imagined,
Will suddenly surge to the surface
And we will recollect and remember
With happiness, pleasure and peace
The lives we have lived.

Twenty Years Later

**Dedicated to those who lost their lives
And to those who live on without them!**

Twenty years later
I still feel an intense sadness
As I remember,
Along with the rest of the world,
All that happened on 9/11/2001,
How our world was forever changed.

That dark day, we lost
A little bit of our freedom
A little bit of our peace
A little bit of our joy
A little bit of our innocence
A little bit of our life,
All gone forever.

So many children
Have grown up
Without their mothers and fathers.
So many husbands and wives
Have continued on
Without their loved ones.
So many people
Have lived on
Without their brothers and sisters.
So many seniors
Have simply existed, gone on
Without their children and
    grandchildren
Gathered around them.
So many lived differently
For the rest of their lives
Touched forever
By that one dark day.

We came together
And we recovered
But we were different.
We were changed forever.
For the impact felt that day
Never fully went away
It still lingers on today
Twenty years later
And always will.

We will never forget
As we remember
Those who were lost
But we must care for those
Who have lived on,
Those who lost so much.

It will always be
Up to each of us
To keep their memories alive,
To help this become a better world,
To live the best lives we can,
To make them proud
Of the people we have become,
To ensure that their memories
Warm our hearts forever.

As A Nation

As a Nation
We are not perfect
But we are respected and loved
By so many people
Around the world
For what we have done
Throughout our history.

As a Nation,
We have made serious mistakes.
Mistakes that have tainted
The very soul of our Nation.
Stains that will never
Be completely removed or forgotten.

As a Nation,
We must never forget,
Never repeat our Past.
We must make changes
To make our Present stronger.
We must move forward
Into our Future together,
Healing and better than ever.

As a Nation,
Despite any shortcomings
We may have
We need to stand proudly
Remembering all the good
We have accomplished together
For no Nation on earth is perfect.

As a Nation,
The History
We will forever live with
Was created by flawed people.
We will learn from their mistakes
But we should not,
Can not and must not
Dwell on the past
As we try to build
A greater future
For all the Generations
Who follow in our footsteps.

I will forever take great pride
In calling myself a Canadian,
Today on Canada Day
And on all other days,
Throughout the years of my life.

For despite our follies,
Our foibles and our weaknesses
We are a good people,
We are a good county,
Standing proud, standing strong
Together building a better tomorrow
As we move forward
Into our future as a Nation.

The Person I Once Was

Dedicated to all Seniors.

Times passes by
So very quickly
As I grow older.
Days, weeks and months
Turn into years and decades
Before I even realize they are gone.

I can't think as quickly,
I do not react as I once did.
I don't remember as well
I'm not able to do things
That in years gone by
Were so easy.

Yet others seem to remember me
As I was twenty and thirty years ago.
They wonder why
I am not the same
As I was back then.

My body does not respond
As it once did.
Small aches and pains
Have become far more debilitating
Than they were years ago.

I can not hear as sharply
As I once did.
I miss words and phrases
In simple, everyday conversations.
My vision is not as strong
Clarity of sight is now blurred.
Some people become frustrated with
    me
But not nearly as much
As I am with myself.

My mind, still active as ever,
Can not recall people and places
Yet I can remember
Even the most insignificant of events
From thirty years ago
Sometimes more easily
Than I do from thirty days ago.

I have to work so much harder
At tasks, once so simple to perform,
Now cloaked with difficulty.
Some people become impatient with
    me
When I am not the person I was,
The one they remember from my past.

I am now closer
To my 70s and 80s
Than to my 40s and 50s,
Even though I may not look my age.
My mind and my body
Remind me daily
I have passed well
Into my sunset years.

Yet so often, other people's perception
    of me
No longer matches the reality of my
    life.
No one can ever be
More frustrated, more impatient,
Less understanding, less
    compassionate
Than I am with myself.
I appreciate and acknowledge
I have to accept the fact
I can not longer do
Many things I once did.
My mind and my body

Will continue to react
More slowly, less actively
As time continues to march on.

I can only hope others
Will be more tolerant,
Will be more patient,
Will be more considerate,
Will be more kind,

As my life continues to change
For I am and will never again be
The person I once was.

Lost Friends

When I reflect on my life,
Thinking back on the memories
Created over many years.
It makes me sad
To think of all the people,
Once so close,
Now distant, gone forever.

No longer friends,
Time and distance severed
The close bonds once held so dear.
Once, so strong,
Torn apart,
Now merely
Fading memories of the past,
Long gone by.

Once, we travelled together
Along the same path
But far too soon
Our lives went in different directions,
Never to be in lockstep again.
As I think back during the sunset of
    my life
Do I have any impact
On the memories of their lives
As they do on mine?

I often wonder if they think of me
As I do of them
Or I was simply a moment gone by?
Lost forever, never revisited.
When I have departed
Will they relive
The times we spent together?
Will they recall
The closeness we shared?

Or were we just
Two ships passing one night
A moment in time lost forever?
Irrelevant, immaterial, unimportant,
A memory set adrift deep within?
I will always remember,
I will refuse to forget,
Keeping alive, protecting and
    preserving
The memories of those lost friends
Who were an important part of my
    life.

Section 4
Gone But Not Forgotten

Gone

Far too soon
I will be gone
But I will be with you.
You will hear me
Whisper in the wind.
You will feel me
In the gentle rain.
You will see me
As a butterfly floats by.

For I will always be here
To guide and protect you
As you walk
Your own pathway through life.

You may feel sadness for a while
But it will fade over time
To be replaced by the joy
Of the memories we created together.

I will be gone
But I will never leave you.
You will hear me
In the sweet laughter of a child.
You will feel me
Deep within your heart.
You will see me
In the beauty of a sunset.

Your life will go on,
Always move forward.
Be happy, be brave, be strong.
Be thankful for all the times we
    shared.

Make me proud in everything you do.
For I will beside you.
You may not see me
But you will know I am there.

I will be gone
But I will be near you.
You will hear me
In your mind.
You will feel me
Close to you.
You will see me
In the beauty of nature.

Far too soon,
I will be gone
So let's enjoy every moment
We have together,
Making the memories
You will always cherish
When I am gone.

I Will Be With You

Tomorrow
When you awaken
I will be gone
But will always
Be near you.

You will not
Be able to see me
With your eyes.
To feel me
With your touch.
To hear me
With your ears.
To speak to me
With your words.

But you will see me
In your memories.
You will feel me
In your emotions.
You will hear me
In your mind.
You will speak to me
In your dreams.

As you complete
Your journey through life
I will walk beside you,
Guiding you along the way,
Watching over you each day.

Tomorrow,
I will be gone
But I will always
Stay near you.

You will see me
In each sunrise and sunset.
You will feel me
In the gentle morning breeze.
You will hear me
In the tune of a songbird.
You will speak to me
In your prayers.

For wherever you go,
Wherever you are.
I will see you.
I will feel you.
I will hear you.
I will speak to you.

All you will have to do is
Look for me,
Reach out to me,
Listen for me,
Speak to me.
For I will always be
Near you, beside you, with you.

Remembering You

Life goes on
But it is so very different
Without you walking each step
Beside me.
You are never far from my thoughts.
There is not a single day that passes
When I do not think of you
Remembering our life together,
Remembering you.

So many little things
Remind me of you.
Sometimes,
A telephone ringing
Or the time of day chiming.
Other times,
The sounds of a thunderstorm
Or listening to a breeze blowing
On a bright sunny day.

Sometimes,
Taking a walk
As a butterfly floats by
Or the sound of a songbird
Calling out to it's mate
In the early morning
Or in the glow of sunset.

Other times,
Sitting quietly,
Reading a book,
Watching television
Or listening to a song
Will trigger a memory.

From time to time,
I will stop for a moment.
I will shed a tear.
But there is always
A warm feeling in my heart
As I remember you.

Life goes on
But it is so very different
Without you walking each step
Beside me.
You are never far from my thoughts.
There is not a single day that passes
When I do not think of you
Remembering our life together,
Remembering you.

Gone but Never Forgotten

It was just
A short time ago
You were taken from us.
When you left, you took
An irreplaceable part
Of us with you.
A part of us
That was yours
And your alone to take.

You lived your life
With such incredible
Passion, commitment and love.
Touching and changing
So many around you
Throughout your short life.

Leaving indelible footprints
On our lives
And in our hearts.
Footprints you will never see,
Remaining hidden,
Deep within us
For the rest
Of our lives.

Wherever you went,
Whatever you did,
Whoever you were with.
Everything in your life
Was filled with
Such passion,
Such commitment,
Such love.

It was quite simply impossible
Not to love
And be loved by you.
We will never be the same
Without you in our lives
But we will always be better
For having had you in them.

You were gone
Far too soon
But you will
Always be remembered
By everyone
You touched and loved
Throughout your life.

As the years pass by
It will never get easier.
We will live on but
Our lives are forever changed.
Never to be
Quite the same
Without you.

You may be gone
But you will never
Be forgotten.
You will live on
In each of us
For the rest of our lives.
Your memory will warm
Our hearts forever.

The Worth of a Man

The worth of a man is not measured
By his possessions or how much
   money
He may have but by
How he is loved by so many after he
   is gone.

He will be judged by the outpouring
   of love,
By the words and memories they
   share
When he is no longer here
To receive, accept and enjoy the
   accolades.

For he will always be remembered
By everyone who felt his love
And the memories he created
When he was here with us.

How many left behind will forever
   feel
He was their brother for life?
How many will remember and honour
   him
Over the many years to come?

How many lives have been forever
   changed
Because he IS no longer part of them?
Yet how many have been forever
   changed
Because he WAS part of them?

He is gone far too soon
Yet he will live on
In the hearts of all
Who knew and loved him.

A dangerous and deadly disease
May have taken him from us
But we are all so much better
For having known him.

The kindness he shared throughout
   his life
Has touched our souls.
His love, his wisdom and his words
Are imprinted within our hearts.

He may be gone
But he will never be forgotten
As the memories of him
Will warm our hearts forever.

The Train Has Left The Station

Dedicated to the memory of my friend,
My fellow cancer warrior, Marke Dally

Life is not fair.
Cancer even less so.

I will miss him forever
But I know his memory
Will always warm my heart.

He fought longer, braver and harder
Than anyone I have
Or will ever know.

Time after time,
He cast aside and defeated
The ugliness of this hideous, insidious
    disease.

But, ultimately,
In an unfair, untimely and unwelcome
    fashion,
After winning battle after battle,
He lost the war.

A war that was totally relentless,
Totally unforgiving,
Totally unfair to him
And all who loved him.

He was the best of friends
To everyone he knew.
He was a brother
To so many of us.

His hugs were like a huge cuddly bear
That completely encircled and
    encompassed you.

They will never be forgotten
By anyone of us who ever
    experienced them.

He would kiss you on the cheek
Without giving a damn
If anyone happened to be watching.

He was kind,
He was knowledgable.

He was honourable,
He was humble,

He was loving,
He was loyal.
Through thick and thin,
Through all the challenges of life,
If you needed him,
He would stand by your side.

Fighting your battles
As if they were his own.
He was as rare a person
As you will ever find.

Life will go on
But it will never be the same
Without his spark of friendship
Lighting the way.

I am and will always be
So very proud and happy
That I was his friend
And he was mine.

Yet so very sad
That the train
Has left the station.

Karen

Dedicated to Karen Carpenter
Taken from us far too soon.

So sweet, so smooth
Yet so sultry, so sexy.
A soft, silky voice
Singing out to the world
About the possibilities and potential
Of love and life.

Watching her was an emotional
    experience
Evoking a calmer, gentler side to our
    lives.
Reaching out and touching everyone
In the throes of a complex world.

She held her audiences transfixed
With her voice and her music.
A voice extinguished far too soon
Leaving so many lyrics unspoken,
So many melodies unsung.

She touched the hearts of a generation
Helping us find our way,
Cleaning, clearing and cleansing
The confusion of our times.
She gave us an alternative,
A mellow, quieter music
During an era of the loud rock music
Throughout the challenging, turbulent
    times.

Even today,
Her music evokes memories
Of a simpler, more innocent time in
    our lives.
An intimacy calling out

Through the melodies,
The harmonies whispering softly
To all of us.

Yet behind the quiet beauty of her
    music
There was always a shadow unseen,
Hidden deep beneath her song and her
    smile
Nothing was said,
So many secrets were kept,
The truth unrevealed, unknown
Until it was too late.

Then, so suddenly, her music died.
She was gone forever
Yet the messages held deep within
Will live on forever.

Gone but never forgotten,
Her ongoing success springs
From the simplicity
Of the words she sang
Within tight harmonies of the music.
Loved by many, missed by all.

Even today, reliving the past,
Watching her recordings,
Listening to her sing
She continues to comfort our souls
And to warm our hearts.

She died so very young
Yet she lives on
In the songs she sang.
The lyrics, the melodies
And the message of love
Will always be "close to us".

Brian Williams: One Great Sportscaster

He made us proud to be Canadians.
He made us happy to be sports fans.
He became our head cheerleader.
He lead us through five decades,
Fifty years of sports.
Fourteen Olympic Games,
Countless Grey Cups
And too many different sports to
    name.

Through the highs and lows
Of all sports over the years,
Speaking to countless athletes
He celebrated their successes
He commiserated their failures
He laughed with them,
He cried with them.
He made sports feel real
To every one of us.

He defined many moments in time
We will remember
For the rest of our lives.
His voice was so welcome,
So well known
In the living rooms and bedrooms
Throughout our country.

He made us feel a part
Of all the sporting events
We were watching.
He helped us understand
The joy and the intricacies of sport.

Though him,
We all became fans.
His kindness, his sincerity,
His honesty, his professionalism
Will be missed
By all Canadian sports fans
But will always be fondly
    remembered.

We will continue to watch,
To participate, to enjoy,
To cheer for our teams
Be it the Olympic Games,
Grey Cups or any of the many sports
He brought into our lives
For five decades.
But it will never be
Quite the same without him.

Donna

From a church choir
To the Last Dance,
From musical theatre
To the infancy of music videos,
From the obscurity of Germany
To the stage of the world.
From Hair to Hot Stuff,
From Gospel to MacArthur Park,
From Rock to Disco.

Through five decades
In a challenging,
Changing and confrontational world,
Breaking down life-long barriers
As she climbed the charts
Into the hearts of millions.
She became, reigned and remained
The Queen of Disco,
The First Lady of Love

Time and again,
Rising from the ashes,
Reinventing herself,
Making mistakes along the way
She learned and grew
As she persevered and overcame
All the roadblocks
Life placed in her path.

She smashed through
The glass ceiling,
She broke down
Generational obstacles,
She opened doors
For others to follow.

Loved by millions
Yet like so many others
Taken well before her time.
She blazed a trail,
Unstoppable,
She sang and danced
Her way to the heights.

Her music became
The soul of a generation
To be shared, listened to and loved
By all generations to follow.
She may be gone
But her music and dance
Live on as a loving legacy and tribute
To her life and times.

Elizabeth, Queen of the World

Dedicated to Queen Elizabeth II
As the World celebrates her
Platinum Jubilee

A small, frail figure
Stands alone on a balcony
Being saluted and cheered
By millions beneath her
With millions more around the world
Watching in awe
With a sense of pride,
Celebrating her incredible
Strength, perseverance and endurance.
Commemorating a truly remarkable
Lifetime of service.

She has reigned for seven decades
Longer than most have even been alive.
Yet they cheer for her and for hope
In a more complex, very different world
From the one she knew
When she ascended to the throne
So many years ago.
She has persevered
Through good times and bad times,
Through war and peace,
Through difficult times of change
Through personal family challenges
Through the heartache
Of personal sacrifice and tragedy.

She has endured and survived
The loneliness of her inheritance,
With the heavy weight of her mantle,
She has ruled with a quiet, calm
    dignity
For the many generations
Who have looked to her
Through ever-changing and
    challenging times.

She has kept the sacred promise and
    oath
She made to them so many years ago.
As age has stolen away
Much of her youthful strength
She has always been tacitly vigilant
In lifelong pursuit of fairness and
    impartiality.
She remains such a familiar figure to
    all.

Avoiding much of the political
    conflict
That has evolved over the decades.
With a sense of grace and decorum
She has taken many recriminations
Thrown at her without descending
Into war of words with her accusers.
Stoically, she has ruled
With a sense of fairness
In an often unfair world.

So, now she stands quietly
As her family gathers around her
She smiles serenely,
Weakly waving to her subjects
Trembling ever so slightly as the
    world
Celebrates the seventy years of her
    reign.

Silently knowing that one day soon
She will pass
The mantle of her office
To the next generation,
Completely secure in the knowledge
She has successfully accomplished
What she set out to do
So many years ago.

Tyre

What has happened to our world?
What have we become?
Where will it all end?

An innocent young man,
Lying, brutally beaten in the darkness,
So close to his home, his safe haven.
Savaged by men sworn
To protect and defend him.

Dying on the cold, hard concrete,
In confusion, fear and disbelief,
Crying out for his mother
When there is soft grass
Just yards away from him.
The street light high above him
Sending down an eerie, flickering
    glow
Casting shadows on his last view of
    the world

Large hulks of thugs in blue uniforms
Hovering above him,
Having just inhumanly,
Without justification, without mercy
Kicked and beaten him.
Not one of them offering him
Any help, any kindness, any solace.

Others have arrived,
Professionals trained
To ease his pain,
To give him comfort,
To save his life
Yet not one of them come to him
To do what they need to do.

His mother, only blocks away,
Unaware, her life was changing
    forever,

Her baby, her son,
Lying in the darkness
Weakly calling out for her.

His neighbours, closing their shutters,
Hiding away, fearing retribution
From the gang in blue,
Standing around, smoking,
Telling each other stories
Creating false fabrications of the
    events
Which will send this young man
Reeling from this life into the next.

Professionals, bound by oath and
    duty,
Leaving him bleeding and in pain,
Fading in and out of consciousness
After the unbelievable, inhumane
    brutality
They have inflicted upon him.
Simply casting large, frightening
    shadows
Above and around him
As his life ebbs away.

He will take his last breath
In a cold, sterile hospital
But he died on that dark,
Dimly-lit street corner.
Without help, without humanity,
Without consideration, without
    compassion,
Without sympathy, without love.

What has happened to our world?
What have we become?
Where will it all end?

Gordon

**Dedicated to a true Canadian,
Gordon Lightfoot**

The troubadour is gone!
He told his stories,
He sang his songs,
He taught us
What it is to be Canadian.

Throughout the decades
Of our childhood,
Of our youth
Of our adulthood,
Through the generations of change
We listened, we learned and we loved
As he sang about our Country.

He inspired us to be better,
To always rise to our potential,
To love and to be proud
Of who we are as Canadians.

His music reached out
And touched our hearts.
He was there
When we needed him.
He helped define us
As a Nation.

He has left us
An anthology of Canadiana
And there will never be another
Just like him.
Yes, the troubadour is gone!
Long live his legacy,
His music and his memory!

Section 5
The Musings of a Poet

Painter or Poet?

A painter creates a picture
One can see with their eyes.
A poet paints a picture
With words that the mind
Must interpret and imagine.

A painter uses
All the colours on his pallet.
A poet creates
His picture using the words
On the pallet of one's imagination.

A painter's picture
Can be seen and touched.
A poet's picture
Must be imagined
Through the imagery of his words.

Both use their imagination
To create their images.
A painter with his hands,
A poet with his words.

There is a wondrous beauty
To behold in both.
One can be physically seen
The other must be envisioned
Through the eyes of the mind.

One is immediate
For it is tangible.
The other takes more time
For it is intangible.

Painter or poet?
Both creating beautiful images
For all of us to enjoy forever
But each does so
In such a completely
Diverse and different way.

A Life Changed

Cancer has changed my life.
From the moment
I received the news
Instead of merely living it
I was fighting for it.

I was just drifting along
But now,
I am riding through life.
Every minute, every moment,
Every day is precious to me.

So many little things
I once took for granted
Are now cherished by me.
Taking time to look,
To really look
At the world around me.

Seeing, feeling, enjoying
All the simple things
Nature has to offer me
Each and every day.

Before cancer
I would just rush along
Barely noticing
The beauty all around me
As I passed by.

Now I take the time
To see the sun, the sky and the clouds,
The trees, the animals and the birds
To enjoy all that nature has to offer.

To feel the warm breezes of summer
And the cold biting winds of winter.
To hear the symphony of sounds
All around me.

No longer am I simply
Passively reacting to life.
I am actively living it
To the fullest
Each and every day.

Never allowing my disease
To control my life
But fighting with my attitude,
With everything I have,
With everything I do
To overcome, control and conquer it.

Yes, cancer has changed my life.
From the moment
I received the news
Instead of merely living it,
I am fighting for it.

One Thread of Happiness

As I fight my inner battle, each and
  every day.
My fear growing, seemingly never
  going away.
My mind allows itself to play a
  sinister game,
Knowing things around me will never
  be the same.

Always hoping and wishing for the
  best
So late at night, I can get some rest.
Waiting and praying for my disease to
  improve
So, at long last, my body and soul will
  sooth.

All the while, knowing it may stay the
  same.
Realizing I may have to live, fighting
  the pain.
It becomes the only way, I surmise
To move ahead and to survive.

At times like this, I feel distressed
Leaving my mind to become
  depressed
All the while understanding, I must
  rise above,
Knowing my family will always share
  their love

Yet, an ongoing sadness fills my heart
As the challenges of life keep us
  apart.
I know one day soon together, we will
  be
But through the darkness, it is so
  difficult to see.

My future remains a question, more
  or less
As I challenge myself to not take on
  more stress.
And so it is, I lie awake late at night
Knowing I will continue to fight

Understanding whatever it is,
  affecting me so
I must win my battle against this foe.
I need to continue on, day by day,
Recognizing step by step, I will have
  my say.

For only I can improve my life
As I fight though all the oncoming
  strife.
For only I can overcome this beast.
To confront and to combat at the very
  least.

Looking to the future becomes my
  best hope
Seeing the days ahead, my only way
  to cope.
So, now at last, I will fall asleep
For this one thread of happiness is
  mine to keep.

Little Things

The little things we do,
The little things we say,
Can change the lives
Of those around us.

There are far too many
In the world today
Living on their own isolated islands
Reluctant to reach out.

Hesitant to help others,
Resistant to change,
Unwilling to make a move
With a small word of encouragement
Or a simple act of kindness.

It is time for us
To leave our islands,
To lend a hand of help
To say a word of inspiration
To create a footprint of change.

In our complicated world
It is the little things
We do and say
That will change the lives
Of those who need it most
When they need it most.

It takes so little to make a big impact.
For even the smallest of pebbles
Thrown into the ocean
Over time will create
Huge waves of transformation.

The time of inertia,
The time of apathy,
The time of indifference
Must come to an end.

The time for action,
The time for empathy,
The time for change
Is here and now!

Each of us
Has an innate ability
Within us to become
Those much needed
Pebbles of change.

With just a kind word
Or a meaningful action
We can move our world
Towards a brighter future.

We need to always remember
It is the little things
We say and do that
Can move mountains,
Will affect attitudes,
And change the world.

Creating Poetry

It begins with a spark of inspiration,
Combined with the fire of imagination
Followed by the free flow of words
Designed to create an empathy
With those who will take the time
To read the poetry, once completed.

Sometimes, easily falling into place,
Often taking more time
To ensure the message is clear and
    concise.
Working and waiting patiently
For thoughts and impressions to
    emerge.

Assembling each word, each line,
    each stanza
Before the poem begins to appear.
Reading and rereading,
Moving ideas and images into place.
Writing quietly with passion in the
    dark of the night.

Letting reflections, perceptions and
    concepts emerge
Without restriction, without limitation
Never fully knowing exactly
What will materialize for the work to
    be completed.
Therein lies the excitement,
The emotion and the anticipation
Of the creative process.

Before long, the pattern of the poem
Begins to to take shape.
The artistry of creating poetry
Is the ability to sense, to recognize
When the best words and phrases
On the page before them are in place
Conveying the true meaning of their
    efforts.

Then, the poet will be ready to share
Their work with the world around
    them
Wanting to initiate and enhance
The enjoyment and emotion of their
    readers
Through the empathy of their words.
Their poetic desire is to uplift and to
    inspire,
To help and to motivate their readers.

Hoping their poetry will be read and
    seen
As a tonic for these turbulent times.
To have their readers walk beside
    them
To see the world as they do,
To share their emotions and
    experiences
In the words they have written.
A poet can ask for nothing more.

A Mirror

A poet is a mirror
Simply reflecting the world
They see around them.
Their words are a microcosm of life.
If you don't like what you read,
Perhaps, it is time
To change the world around you.

Status quo is not a good thing.
We need to adapt, to change
As our environment evolves.
We need to become more flexible
As life unfolds before us.
The path we are following is
    developing
As we move along it.

One day will never the the same
As the day before it,
Always different
From the day that follows.
A poet's words will embody
Their view shrouded with empathy,
Revealing the world as it is.

If we want
A poet's message to change
We need to revise
What they are seeing around them.
Like a mirror,
They are simply showing you
The world as it is.

Six

The number six has such a bearing on
    our lives
Just a simple number but so much
    more
For all of us, never knowing what lies
    in store!

It took only six seconds to kill a
    President,
Three quick shots by Lee Harvey
    Oswald
Forever changed our world

Six feet apart during the pandemic
To stay away, to inspire us
To survive and fight this virus.

Six feet under when we die
Buried with dignity and respect
Something while living we often
    reject.

Six wives of King Henry
"Divorced, Beheaded, Died
Divorced, Beheaded, Survived"

Six feet tall
As a man stands proud
Living life within the crowd.

Sixth sense
To be aware beyond the norm
To perceive life in a different form.

The birth of sextuplets
Celebrated as something rare
Creates a family with none to
    compare.

The Star of David with six points
    flying high
Representing a country filled with
    proud folk
Throughout history bravely bearing
    their yoke.

Many sports teams compete with six,
Always playing to be the best
To win the cup, the bowl or the crest.

The number six has such a bearing on
    our lives
Just a simple number but so much
    more
For all of us, never knowing what lies
    in store.

These Are The Things

I will never apologize to anyone.
For these things are the only way
I know how to battle
The disease within me.

Writing and sharing my poetry
To keep my mind active.
Riding my bike every day
To keep my body active.

Walking my puppies
To rest my weary soul.
Watching nature all around me,
Witnessing an early morning sunrise
Or an evening sunset.

Raising money
To help those organizations
Who help other cancer warriors
Continue to fight their battles.

The people I ask to help me,
A large circle of friends
Gathered from a lifetime of activity
Can always say no.

But that will never deter me
To continue the battle,
To travel the course
I have chosen!

I hope it will not
Affect our relationship
For asking is not demanding,
It is simply asking.
The choice to help me is theirs
And theirs alone to make.

These are the things
I must continue to do.
They are ingrained
Deep within me,
For they are an integral part
Of the new life
I have been forced to adopt.

These are the things
I totally believe in
With all of my heart.

These are the things
That will help me
To continue to fight
The battle I must fight.

Always accepting and believing,
It is what it is!
One step at a time!
One day at a time!

We All Matter

We all matter.
Black, white
Brown, yellow.
Put away the hatred!
Put away the rhetoric!
Put away the politics!
Put away the guns!

We all matter.
Let's learn to live with one another.
Let's learn to accept one another.
Let's learn to be more tolerant of one
    another.
Regardless
Of our different beliefs,
Of our different lifestyles,
Of our different social values

We all matter.
Each of us
Has someone who loves us,
Has someone we love.
Each of us
Has a purpose in life,
Our dreams, our aspirations
Our reasons for living.

We all matter.
Each of us
Living though different stages in our
    lives.
As children and teenagers,
As adults and seniors.
The older we are
The more stages we have experienced.

We have faced different challenges,
We have overcome different
    obstacles,
We survived many different struggles
We all need to be
More understanding of others
At different stages in their lives.

We all matter.
Life is the journey
We are taking together
On this small blue planet
In the infinite universe surrounding
    us.
Different stages, different
    experiences,

But in the end,
We will all be the same.
So why not share more love,
More patience, more empathy.
Always remembering,
We all matter.

The Ass's Tale

One rainy day,
The donkey cried out to the heavens
" All the other animals are
So much better off than me.
They live truly wonderful lives!
I wish I could be one of them! "

A heavenly voice called down
" Donkey, why would you want that?
You are perfect.
Your life is perfect, just as it is! "

The donkey replied
"But look at the horse.
Man can ride on his back.
He performs so many tasks.
He is so stately and beautiful.
Man truly loves him!"

"Look at the eagle, so majestic,
Flying high above the earth
Able to see the whole world from
    above!
While I am here
Stuck on the ground
Just plodding along through the mud
Unable to see beyond the next bend in
    the road."

"Look at the Dog
Loved by every person
Who lives with one.
So faithful, so dedicated
Always seen as
"Man's best friend.""

"Look at the Sheep
Grazing quietly, day after day,
Living free in the fields.

Providing wool,
Year after year,
To keep Man warm
During the cold winter nights."

"Look at the Cow,
Providing milk and meat
To help Man sustain himself.
In some cultures,
They are even worshipped."

"Even snake has his place.
Slithering silently and stealthily
Along the ground
Cleaning up the vermin
That could create disease
Which would hurt Man."

After the heavenly voice
Had quietly listened
He spoke softly and kindly
To the Donkey

"Be careful what you wish for.
For you are perfect as you are.
Just think,
You are the only one
In the world who can get away
With being a complete ass
For ALL of your life.

For I created you
To be and do just that!
Some Men will try to copy you
And will be seen as Asses
But they are simply cheap imitations
For only you
Can truly get away with it."

On another day, not long after,
The Donkey decided
To go for an walkabout
To discover for himself how well
All the other animals lived.
Then, he would finally have proof
As to how badly off he really was.

First he stopped at a farmer's field
Where a horse was working in the
    field
Hitched to a heavy plow.
"Hey, horse" called out the donkey
" What are you doing?
I thought horses just rode
With people on their back
Who loved them. "

" Well, my friend,
You are sadly mistaken.
Many of us have to work like this
For most of our lives.
It is a hard life which wears us out
And we die young.
There is no escape for us! "

Feeling a little sorry for the horse,
The donkey looked up to the sky
As he walked on and called out to the
    Eagle
" You are so lucky to be able to fly
So high above the earth,
Looking as majestic as you do!"

" No, my friend"
The Eagle called back
" I am not lucky.
I miss all that is happening
Down on the ground
Soaring so high above
And Man shoots at us with his guns
So the skies are never safe. "

Again, the Donkey walked on
And met a poor, bedraggled, hungry
    dog
Lying forlornly the side of the road
" Why are you not with your Man
Being fed and cared for?"

The Dog lifted his tired head
" There are only a few of us
Who live that kind of life.
So many more are like me.
Homeless, hungry and unloved
Scrounging for food,
Day in and day out.
Living life as best we can
Waiting for the Rainbow Bridge to
    call us home! "
Sadly, the Donkey left the dog
And walked on.
Before long, he met the sheep
Grazing unhappily in the field.
The Donkey called out
"Why are you so sad?
You have a woolly coat
To keep warm on cold mornings,
You have a home and lots of food"

The Sheep sadly said
" You do not understand.
The warm coat is only mine
Until Man decides to shear it off
Just before the cruel winter ahead.
If, for any reason, my coat
Does not grow as thick and luscious
As Man would like,
My life will be over at his whim
As I will fill his stomach instead. "

As the Donkey walked on
He thought to himself
"How could I have been
So wrong about all these animals".
Then, he spotted a cow
Grazing the field beside the road
"I am sure his story
Will be much better"

He called out to the Cow
"Tell me about the wonderful life you
    lead"
The Cow quietly said
"What wonderful Life?
If we are lucky,
We are used only for our milk.
Otherwise, we feed Man.
It is no life at all!
Just a lonely and undignified end for
    us!"

Suddenly, a snake peaked out at the
    donkey
From the tall grass by the roadside.
"Surely, your life is better than the
    Cows"
The Snake hissed unpleasantly.
" What makesss you sssay that?"
The Donkey thought for a moment
"You are free to slither wherever you
    want.
You know no boundaries. You live
    free. "

The Snake responded
" Maybe ssso but we are hated by all
And hunted by a few.
Without warning, the Eagle
    ssswoopsss down
And our life is sssuddenly and quickly
    over!
We know no peaccce!
It isss not a good life we live!"

So, after all this, the Donkey
    discovered
The life he led was not as bad
As he had always thought!
He could live like an Ass
And no one thought the worse of him.
He was neither abused, eaten or
    hunted.
In fact, he lived in peace.
So, he decided he would be more than
    happy
To live like an Ass for the rest of his
    life!

Finding An Inner Peace

Beyond the window
The wind is howling,
The day, dark and stormy,
Yet, we sit here
Warmed by the glow of the fire.
Safeguarded
From the ravages of the nature
Protected
From the travails of the outside world.

Peaceful and contented,
We sit quietly
Sheltered
From the uncontrolled chaos beyond.
Our relaxed minds create
A stark contrast
To the pandemonium raging around
   us.
Our inner sanctum
Provides a safe cocoon
Insulating us from the reality
Seen and heard outside.

Yet, at other times
We live with an inner turmoil
Our minds and bodies,
So conflicted,
Fighting unseen demons
Struggling to understand why
While the sun is shining
On a clear, beautiful day
Spreading warmth all around us
As nature peacefully rests
We wage an unnecessary, internal war

Will we ever find
A peaceful serenity within
As nature does the same?
Perhaps, this is one of
Life's ongoing challenges.
Finding that ability
To enjoy an inner peace,
A calm within
Matching nature outside.

Wounded

We are all wounded,
Some just a little,
Others more than a little.
Some wounds are external,
Seen by the eye,
Others are internal,
Hidden away from the outside world.

Those which can be seen
Are usually easier to fight.
It is the unseen and unknown
We are challenged to face
Throughout of our lives.
Those wounds must not be ignored
Or they will fester
Growing worse over time.

We need to be ready
To recognize and challenge our
    wounds
In order to fight them,
In order to manage them,
In order to overcome them.

For the sake
Of our health and our sanity
The more we know,
The better it will all be.
Enabling us to fight the battles
We know must be fought.

The mental ones are often
More difficult to fight
Than the physical ones.
Yet they are as important to combat
And must not be ignored.
For they will not simply go away,

Each and every day,
The struggle will continue.
There may be changes over time
But the battle will continue
For a lifetime.

Knowledge and communication
Are the tools needed
To wage the war
Against the hidden enemy.
The more we know,
The stronger we become.
The more we openly communicate,
There will be others who will help us.

Whether the wounds are
Physical, mental or spiritual,
We need to know
We are not alone.
For with the help of others,
The wounds will change over time.
We need to understand
The healing process will be a long
    one.

As long as we are prepared
To face and accept
The challenges before us
Always moving forward,
Ready to fight,
Ready to overcome,
Ready to heal,
Knowing we are never alone,
Knowing we are all wounded.

Waiting

Written during another layover in another airport.

Waiting,
We always seem to be waiting
For our next adventure to begin.
I want to be doing something
To be active,
To be part of my next life experience.
Not simply sitting here
Until our next flight departs.

Time passes so very slowly.
The seconds
Feel like intolerable minutes,
The minutes
Like unending hours,
The hours
Become unspeakable lonely mental
    torture.

There must be something
I can do to pass the time
As mine-numbing boredom sets in.
Why can't I just be satisfied?
Sleeping quietly in a chair
Like the puppy beside me.
No concept of time,
No worries about when we will leave.
Just perfectly content
To be lying quietly.

Why do I feel
I should always
Be doing something?
Each of us have the same
Amount of time every day.
Why do some people use
Their time so much better than others?

Perhaps,
It is time to relax
My mind and body
Rather than anxiously worrying
About my next activity,
My next adventure,
My next flight.
If my puppy can do it so easily
Surely I can be like him.

Yet my mind and my pulse
Race faster and faster
As I suffer the monotony
Of simply sitting.
As the tediousness of time
Passes so very slowly
While we continue to wait.

What can I do
Alleviate the humdrum mundane
    cycle
That has entrapped me?
How can I escape
The burden of this dull sameness
Currently encircling my existence?

Perhaps,
Simply writing these words
Will be all I need to escape
This wearisome world of waiting.
For now, at last,
The time has come
For us to move again.
As the puppy stirs and awakens,
We will finally walk away
From the tedium of waiting
Back into the reality of life.

Just a Few

Throughout the stages of my life,
People will come and people will go.
For everyone makes their own choices
As we walk the paths of our journey.

So many will pretend
To be my friend
Yet will prove to be false and fleeting.
There will be but a few
Who will always remain true.

They will be the ones
Who like and accept me
For what I am,
For what I have been,
For what I will become.
Quite simply, they like me for me.

These are the people
I want to spend my life getting to
    know.
These are the people
I want to walk beside to the end.
These are the people
I know will always be there
For me and me for them.

Many others will fade in and fade
    away
But these few will remain
A permanent part of the painting
My life is creating,
I can no longer worry about the many
When I will always have the few.

It is time to let go of the many
While holding fast to the few.
Putting the many out of mind
While building close bonds with the
    few.
When I reach the end of my journey
It will be those who I want by my
    side,
To remember me when I am gone.

For when I look back on my life
It will only take a few
To make me smile,
To make me feel joy,
To make my life complete.

Life's Little Things

There will always be aches and pain
But we must move beyond them.
We need to live in the moment.
Enjoying the little things in life.
For in the end, it will be those
We will remember.
For they will be what
Makes our lives complete.

An early morning walk
Watching a beautiful sunrise.
Seeing nature all around us.
The birds, the animals and the
    flowers,
Small ponds surrounded by trees.
A puppy's bark, a child's laugh,
A friend's greeting,
A smile and a hug,

Holding hands with a loved one.
The warm sun shining down,
The gentle breeze blowing,
Running barefoot through the wet
    grass
After a thunderstorm.
Watching a sunset at the end of the
    day,
Sitting quietly in the dark,
Listening to the sounds of the night.

All the major events of our lives
We always thought were so important
Will fade away,
Leaving us to remember
Those simple things
We didn't even think about at the
    time.
Once taken for granted
But in the end,
It will be those
We will recall with happiness.

The River

Your life flows like a river.
Once the water passes by you
It continues somewhere downstream
And becomes your past.
No matter how you try,
You will never catch it again.
The current is always moving
    forward,
Unpredictable and ever-changing.

Your future is somewhere in the
    distance.
Upstream, unknown, unpredictable.
Always flowing forward to meet you.
Then, as quickly as it appears,
It will be gone
And become a part of your past.

Your present is fleeting,
Only with you for a moment
It will be what you make of it.
Take it in, enjoy it,
Make the most of it.
For now is the time
To create the memories
You will want to remember in the
    future
When they are far downstream.

The river, like your life, is constant,
Powerful and always moving forward.
Simply a series of fleeting moments,
Here and, then, gone forever.
Forever moving further away from
    you
Becoming the memories
You will cherish
As you live your life today.

Section 6
Nature

Nature's Serenity

Sitting quietly
On a granite boulder wall
Above the water's edge.
Ferns all around me
Growing out of the rocks
Creating a luscious green carpet,
Seemingly tumbling down the rocks
To the edge of the water.

The sun warming my face
While a cold wind blows
Against my back,
A true contradiction of nature,
Stirring up the lake, ever-changing
From blue to green to grey.

The dark colours of the water
Contrasting with the deep azure blue
Of the cloudless sky above.
As the wind dances
Across the waves it is creating,
I listen to the steady rhythmic sound
Of the waves gently lapping
Onto the shore.

In the distance
A couple of fishing boats
Bobbing and weaving
Between the waves.
Fishing rods,
Moving up and down,
In tune with the rhythmic rocking
Of the boats.

Nearby, two small boys
Racing in kayaks,
Competing with each other
While struggling against
The wind and the waves.

A young couple fishing
On the wet shoreline rocks
Bracing themselves against the breeze
To maintain their balance.
Not worried about catching anything
More there to enjoy each other's
    company.

The branches of the trees around me
Rustling as the wind blows
Through the leaves.
Seagulls floating high above
On the wings of the wind
Searching for their meal
In the murky waters below.

The smell of smoke permeates the air
As a camp fire burns near by.
The warm acrid smell
Quickly passes by,
Not lingering very long ,
Before it is blown away.

Children's happy voices can be heard
As they play at the water's edge.
Their mother straining
To hear them above the wind
Ever watchful, ensuring they stay safe.
As they gleefully shout
Back and forth to one another.

Gazing across the lake,
Watching the peaceful and tranquil
    serenity
Which abounds in this rugged
    landscape,
One that remains untouched by man.
As far as the eye can see
Tall pines line the rocky shore,
Constantly swaying in the relentless
    wind.

As I continue to enjoy nature
In complete synchronization
With the world around it,
I relax in the warmth of the sunlight.

Enjoying the peace and serenity
Of the natural beauty all around me
Before I am forced to return,
Once again, to the civilized world.

The Scents Of Morning

Early in the morning,
Our house is filled with
The aroma of coffee brewing,
Bacon and eggs sizzling in a pan
And newly-made toast.

Then, as I ride my bike,
I enjoy the sweet essence
Of lilac bushes, cherry blossoms
And lavender growing wild in the
    fields.
The crisp, cool air enveloping me
After a sudden summer storm
Or the clean freshness
Of an early morning dew.

I savour the sweetness
Of recently mown grass.
Taking delight
In the gentle bouquet
Of the roses, tulips and tiger lilies
Growing in the gardens
And carried along on the breeze.

These are the scents
Of a morning awakening
I will always remember.
Taking me back
To a gentler, more innocent
And peaceful time in my life.

End of Day

The bright, shining, incandescent orb
Seems to hang motionless
In the western sky.
The clouds surrounding it
Gently glowing, lighting up the sky
As it sinks lower and lower.

With reflections, brightly mirrored,
Across the water of the bay.
The breeze creates
A spectacular shimmering effect
With ripples moving outwards,
Spreading and illuminating,
A rich magical colourful glow
From the water to the land to the sky

As the orange orb slowly sinks
Towards the horizon,
It appears to join
The reflections in the water
And the colours change
To various shades of crimson

The clouds now take on
A phosphorescent glimmer
As another day peacefully
Comes to an end.
The water and the clouds,
Shimmering in shadows,
As the colours continue to change
Moment by moment,
From orange to red to scarlet.

Quite suddenly,
The sun sinks from sight
Below the horizon.
No longer visible to the eye
But sending it's warm radiant glow
High into the heavens above.

The sky now dances
With an ever-changing
Array of colours
Wrapped in an intriguing series
Of delightful patterns.

But only for a few brief minutes
As before long
The shadows and the darkness
Take over, covering everything.
This wondrous display of nature
Quickly, without warning,
Comes to an end.
Leaving the world hidden
In the black cloak of night.

Overnight

Overnight
My world has changed.
The warm breeze of summer
Transformed to the cool wind of fall.
The luscious green foliage
Covering the trees has altered
To a yellow, quickly thinning
    umbrage,
Constantly falling to the ground
    beneath.

The bright blue sky has become
A murky grey covering of clouds,
As the sun has disappeared from view.
The mirror-like aquamarine of the bay
Has turned to a fury of waves,
Stirring the water to a muddy brown.

Just yesterday, wearing shorts
Resting in the warm sunlight.
Now, fully-covered protecting me
Against a changed chilly
    environment.

The geese gathering
In the grass and on the bay
Ready to leave for the winter
On the long trek south.

Other birds and animals,
Not a sound to be heard,
Now hidden from view
Waiting, preparing
For the cold season ahead.

Overnight
My world has changed
As Fall has arrived,
A prelude to Winter
Not far behind.

Poets at Heart

We are all poets at heart.
Yet only a few will communicate
Their vision and their emotions,
Opening themselves up,
Painting a picture with words
And sharing their feelings
With the rest of the world.

Who has not beheld the beauty
Of watching a glorious sunset,
Of the sky and the land
As the world explodes
Into a rainbow of colours
At the end of the day?

Who has not seen
The sun as it rises
Slowly above the eastern horizon,
As the world awakens
Turning from the black blanket of
    night
To the shroud of grey of early
    morning
To the full array of colours
As another day breaks?

Who has not gazed to the night sky
And been a silent witness
To a million twinkling stars
Or watched in wonder
At the dazzling brilliance
Of the dancing Northern Lights?

Or walked along a trail in the woods
As the seasons change,
Seeing the leaves come to life
In the spring

Or silently fall and cover the ground
In the fall
As one rustles along the path
Before the snow falls
To transform the world
In a wonderful blanket of white?

Who has not felt the sensation
As first snowflakes of winter
Landing on their face,
Melting on their cheeks
As the new snowy layer
Crunches beneath their feet.

Who has not experienced the joy
Of seeing the first robin in spring
As the last remnants
Of the winter's snow melts away?
Who has not observed beavers
As they work day and night
Throughout the spring and summer
Building their home
Of mud and branches
Creating a lake
Where only a river ran before?

Or watched mallard ducks
Raising their young in the warm
    waters
Of the bay in the heat of summer?
Who has not admired the elegance
Of the great blue heron
As it stoically stands guard over it's
    nest
Hidden in the bulrushes near the
    shore?

Or the incredible sight
Of hundreds of geese flying in
    formation
On a cool windy autumn day
As they begin their annual trek south?
Or seeing squirrels scurry,
Hither and yon,
As they endlessly gather supplies
For the long, cold winter ahead?

As we witness the world around us,
We are all poets at heart.
Yet only a few will communicate
Their vision and their emotions,
Opening themselves up,
Painting a picture with words
And sharing their feelings
With the rest of the world.

Enjoy the Rainbow

When a storm
Comes to an end
A beautiful rainbow
Appears in the sky
Signalling hope
And new beginnings
For all of us.

The bounty of it's colours
Brings a sense of joy
To all who observe
This wonder of nature.
We are filled with anticipation,
Looking forward
To the future ahead of us.

The colours signifying
So much more
Than meets the eye
And soothes the restless soul.
Representing all of nature
Found beneath the rainbow.

The red
Is the scarlet of robins breast
In the early spring.
It is the wild strawberries
Growing in the garden
It is a beautiful ruby gemstone
Reflecting in the sunlight.

The orange
Is a freshly picked peach,
And the pumpkins on the vine
At Halloween.
It is the tangerine
Of a salmon, strongly swimming
Against the current of a river.

The yellow
Is a bowl of ripe bananas and lemons
Sitting in sun on a kitchen table.
It is golden flaxen hair
Of a young girl, skipping alone,
Under the warm summer sun.

The green
Is a carefully chosen evergreen,
Freshly cut for Christmas,
Waiting to be decorated.
It is the leafy blanket
Covering all the trees
Throughout the spring and summer.

The blue
Is the bright cobalt of the sky
On a frigid winter's day.
It is the aquamarine of the ocean
Stretching out of sight
Towards the far horizon.

The indigo
Is cerulean blue
Found in a newborn's eyes.
It is the teal
On so many beautiful
Tail feathers of a peacock

The violet
Is the lilac bush
Blooming in the spring time.
It is the lavender
Covering the fields in the summer.
Their sweet fragrances
Being carried on the wings of the
    wind.

We need to always remember
To take the time
To stop and relax
Amid the storms of everyday life

During a moment of peaceful solitude
To enjoy the rainbow.

On the Verge of Change

At four different times every year
We are on the verge of change
As nature transitions
From one season to the next.

As the snow and ice melt
As the buds on the trees start to show,
As the birds and animals appear
After being hidden away for so long,
As the world changes from brown to
  green
And the warmth of the sun
Replaces the chill in the air.
We are on the verge of change
As winter transitions to spring.

As the days grow warmer and longer,
As animal and bird babies appear
In nests and shelters.
As the trees and bushes
Are covered in their leafy cloak.
As the river flows freely by.
As flowers and blossoms bloom,
As the world is adorned with bright
  colours,
We are on the verge of change
As spring transitions to summer.

As the warm summer breeze
Transforms into a cool wind.
As the colours on the trees
Adorn the countryside
Then, start to fall away,
Laying bare the branches,

Creating a carpet covering the ground.
As the geese and other birds
Start to gather and prepare for their
  trek south.
As the animals gather food
And build their hideaways
Preparing for the cold times ahead.
We are on the verge of change
As summer transitions to autumn.

As storm clouds gather
And the cold wind blows.
As the rain turns to snow
And the world is
Camouflaged with white.
As all of nature hides away
As the sounds of autumn
Becomes the silence of winter.
As animals and birds forage
For any food they can find.
We are on the verge of change
As autumn transitions to winter.

Before long,
The deep freeze of winter winds
Will begin to grow warmer.
The ice and snow will melt.
Nature will awaken from her long
  sleep.
Animals and birds will reappear.
Muted colours will brighten.
Once again,
As one season transitions to the next,
We are on the verge of change.

The Hunter

As the last shards of light
Disappear into the shadows of the
    night,
The haunting hoot of an owl
Can be heard echoing
In the ever-growing darkness.

His large shadowy outline
Seen on a turret high above us.
The sight and sound of him
A warning to all small creatures
To take refuge, to hide away
From this hungry hunter.

For he will strike, without warning,
Silently swooping toward the ground
Sharp talons ready, poised
To clutch an unsuspecting victim
Returning to his perch
High in the sky
For his evening meal.

Soon the murky shadows
Will hide him from our sight
The darkness making him
An even more dangerous hunter.
Although we can no longer see him
He continues to hunt,
Unseen but seeing all.

Silently watching,
Constantly observing all movement
With clear vision and perception.
In total blackness,
Now shielding him from sight,
Awaiting his moment to strike.

Only his eerie sound
Continues to echo
Throughout the night.
Reminding us he is still there
Perched high in the sky
Patiently waiting,
Continuing to hunt
In the dark shadows below.

In the Garden

As I sit quietly basking in the morning
    sun,
The garden around me glows in the
    early light,
Covered with an overnight dew.
The old cedar and the newly planted
    lavender bushes
Hide me from an awakening world.
Their sweet aromas filling the
    morning air
With a fresh and delightful mixture of
    fragrances.

The healing power of the aloe plants
Spread their tentacles over the wood
    chips
Covering the ground at my feet.
As the sun rises above the building
    near me,
A small lizard sits quietly on one of
    their prongs.
Joining me, enjoying the early
    morning heat
At the beginning of a new day.

I hear a constant buzzing of bees
Continually flying near me,
Carefully landing on the claret red
    flowering cacti
Avoiding the thorny branches.
The deep plum of the wandering Jew
And the majestic violet of the
    persimmon plants
Spread their delightful dew-filled
    colour,
Blanketing the ground around me.

A small rose bush in the corner
It's beautiful blossoming buds
Radiating a delightful tangerine
    orange
As the sun shines down.
An olive green peperomia
Adds an opulent plushness
To my daybreak surroundings.

The luscious leafy shades of basil and
    thyme
Fill the garden, soon to be picked,
Bringing delicious flavours to the
    dishes
Being prepared for our dinner.
As I sip my morning cup of coffee
Relaxing and enjoying
The warmth of the glowing sun
With the scents of enticing aromas,
And the beautiful rainbow of dazzling
    colours
In the vast array of the flora
    surrounding me.

Fingerprints in the Morning

Every morning, I watch in wonder
As the sun rises on the eastern
   horizon.
Realizing in the moment
Each one is an individual fingerprint
Painted on the sky above me.
Unique and unrepeatable,
Distinctive and different
From all the rest.

As the world around me springs to life
Awakening from the slumber of the
   night.
The dark shadows disappear
Replaced by an reddish orange glow
Radiating off buildings and trees.
Reflecting in the early morning light
Bringing joy to my heart.
The dew-covered ground
Shines and sparkles
Giving a surreal shimmering effect.

Always touching my soul,
Relaxing my mind,
Regenerating my body,
Preparing me for the journey ahead.
I feel an inner peace
As the troubles of my world
Are put aside, quietly watching,
This miracle of nature unfold before
   me.

The beginning of a new day,
The rebirth and renewal of life
Always offering me
The opportunity to start again,
To wipe clean the slate of the past
To create a new painting of the
   present
To give hope for the dream of the
   future.

The Lonely Sandhill

The haunting cry of the lonely crane
Echoes though the morning mist.
Her lifetime mate is gone,
Suddenly disappeared overnight.
She endlessly calls out,
Waiting for an answer.

Time and again,
Early cach morning
As her perpetual search continues.
Always the same,
Whether on the ground
Or circling high above.

Her plaintive cries echo non stop
Across the sky to the ground below.
Followed by a sad silence without
    response.
One cannot help
But share in her desolate desperation.

A sense of sadness
Fills the air
As she continues to search
The world around her.
She will never stop.
She is confused.
She is inconsolable
For her life is incomplete
Without her mate.
And so her pleading cry
Continues to echo endlessly
Throughout the day.

The Calm After The Storm

An ominous predawn grey fills my
    room
As the branches outside my window
Sway and dance wildly in the wind.
The world around me is in dark
    shadow
As continuous flashes of lighting
Erupt and fill the sky.

While in the distance
The low rumble of thunder
Builds in intensity as the storm
    approaches.
The puppy beside me sleeps
    contentedly
Ignoring the fury of nature as it
    unfolds.

I watch and listen in muted
    anticipation.
As the thunder rumbles louder than
    before.
The branches stop their pre-storm
    waltz
Within minutes,
Like the sound of a train quickly
    approaching,
I can hear the roar of the rain begin.

Then, as suddenly as it all began
The storm subsides and dissipates
Replaced by an eerie silence.
The thunder, the lightning and the rain
    pass by
The sky begins to brighten
As I wait for the dawn to appear.

Just as in our lives, the wild storm
Leaves behind a peaceful serenity and
    tranquility.
It is the calm after the storm
And life continues with the hope
Of a brighter day ahead.

Watching the Unknown

Millions of shimmering, twinkling
   lights
Flickering like tiny candles
Glowing in the vast expanse of the
   night sky.
So many hidden worlds,
Unknown and unexplored,
So many truths unspoken,
Never to be discovered.

A solitude of silence surrounds me
As I gaze up into the incredible dark
   void.
A peaceful sense of serenity
   envelopes me
As I look at the incredulous sight
Unfolding high above me.

Mankind, in our self-centred,
Self-absorbed, self-righteous mindset,
Somehow believing we are alone
In this grand vastness of space.
Our self-imposed sense of importance
With so many other unknown
   universes
Existing around us.

Our planet is but a tiny blue-green
   marble
Dwarfed by the immense firmament
   surrounding us.
There are innumerable worlds
We will never know,
Never be able to explore,
Never fully understand.

The mystery of the heavens will
   remain
Untouched, unblemished, unspoiled
Throughout the millennia ahead.
Something we can see with our eyes
But will never fully comprehend with
   our minds.
Our world, our universe is just one of
   so many.

Lingering for a moment longer
I stare into the darkness
Seeing but a few of the worlds
   beyond,
Feeling the majesty of the sky,
Filled with a sense of wonder
Watching the unknown.

The Red Ball

The red ball,
Glowing brightly
As it fills the sky
With a shimmering rainbow of colour,
Reflecting across the bay towards me.

I watch the glistening water
As ducks float by
Quietly preparing for the night ahead.
No words are needed
To describe the wondrous beauty
That my eyes behold.

I gaze in wonder
As nature paints
A magical, magnificent picture
At the end of the day.

As each minute passes,
The sky becomes
An even more radiant canvas
With the red ball
Painting a new image to behold,
Captivating and delighting my
    imagination.

All the troubles of the world
Melt away as I watch
The spellbinding scene before me.
There is not a sound
To be heard as the wind
Has come to a standstill.
The cornucopia of colours
Spreads out before me.

The glowing green of the dewy grass
Under my feet,
The effervescent, bright crimson of
    the sky
Above me,
The shadowy, mysterious grey
Of the flickering water,
Hiding so many secrets
Beneath it's surface.

There are ever-encroaching shadows
Gathering around me
As the red ball
Descends behind the line of dark trees
And kisses the western horizon.

Before long,
It will disappear from sight
Taking with it
The wonderful spectacle
I have been witnessing.
Yet for this single moment
I can savour and enjoy
The incredible beauty of the painting
Nature has created.

The Golden Silence

As the dazzling yellow orb rises
Above the trees in the east
A golden glow spreads
Across the bay.
The flaxen bullrushes shining
    luminously
In the early morning light
Creating the perfect picture
Of the harvest season.

The dewy amber blanket of morning
    moisture
Covering everything on the ground
As the warm rays melt
The darkness of the night.
The cool air lingers around us
As we walk along.
The heat of the autumn sun
Not yet warming the world beneath.

The trees, glimmering splendidly
Radiating the early morning light
As the sun catches
The yellow shadows of the few leaves
Remaining on their branches.
Many more gathered on the ground
Scattered around them like a
    shimmering skirt
Ready to protect their bare branches
From the frigid winter ahead.

The multitude of geese
Has gathered throughout the night
Now lying quietly on the ground
Slow to awaken on this frosty
    morning.
Training flights soon to begin
Along with the clamouring noise
Synonymous with their movement.

The bay, motionless,
Without a breath of wind
To disturb it's tranquil serenity.
Shining in the light of daybreak
Like a mirror reflecting the scenes
Along it's shores.
Only later will the water spring to life
As the breeze starts to blow.

The almost unheard footsteps of the
    puppies
With their sniffing of endless
    exploration
Are the only sounds disrupting
The golden silence of the early
    morning
Creating a trail of footprints
Along the soggy shoreline.
Soon to disappear as the sun
Dries the dampened ground
And the world awakens to greet
    another day.

The New Season

There is a feeling of renewal and
    rebirth
In the cool and crisp air
As the world awakens
From it's long slumber,
At long last shedding
It's winter wear.

The sun, shining brightly,
With a warmth, long forgotten,
Shaking loose the dormancy
That has held the world transfixed
Through those many cold months.

Life will soon awaken and begin
    anew
For now, unseen,
Concealed and shrouded,
As the wind blows away
The last vestiges of a season gone by.

The trees, remain for a brief period,
Bare and barren, swaying gently,
Keeping the rhythm of a changing
    time,
Before long to be brilliantly adorned
With pink and purple blossoms

There is a sense
Of regeneration and change
As the green of spring replaces
The white of winter.
As a warmth replaces the cold,
As the frigid sounds
Become melodious melodies.

As people and animals
Emerge refreshed from their cocoons,
Excited and ready
To embrace the change.
Greeting each
After the long hiatus,
Hidden away from one another.

It is a time of rejuvenation,
A time of resumption,
A time of awakening.
As the world around
Advances towards the new season,
Moving away from winter
Transforms into spring.

Section 7
Taking Walks

Watching as the World Awakens

The gentle breeze ripples
Through the bullrushes
At the water's edge.
Small movement begins
On and beneath the water
As another day beckons.

The early morning remains cool
As the heat has yet to emerge.
An azure blue sky
Replaces the dark blanket
Of the night.

Boats remain moored
In their place, floating,
Keeping time to the rhythm of the
    river
As their owners linger
Just a little longer in their beds.

A morning dove coos
While a crow cackles
Endlessly in the distance.
Swallows, diving back and forth,
Gathering for their nests.
A hawk soars gracefully
High overhead
Searching for it's morning meal.

A flag waves gently in the wind
Over the worn and weathered well
Standing guard, covering
A deep supply of water
As it has for so many years.

I sit back, reflecting
In this ever-so-peaceful
Corner of the world
Separated from the turmoil and
    troubles
Surrounding our lives.

For here, in this place,
There is a peaceful solitude
Which relaxes any troubled soul.
I gaze out over the water,
As birds and other wildlife
Float by, unaware of being
So closely watched.

Unafraid, in their undisturbed natural
    habitat
For in this desolate area
Man has co-existed with them for
    years.
So much out here has been left,
Untouched and unchanged,
Allowing nature to thrive and grow.

As the wind picks up
The trees and shrubs begin
Their beautiful, endless dance.
So quiet, so peaceful, so relaxing,
The wind, the water and the birds
All reveal nature as it's finest
As I sit and watch
The world awaken for another day.

Walking Along the River

As I walk along the river
Never knowing when or where
Wonders of nature will appear,
Waiting patiently for the magic
To unfold before my eyes.

A flash of silver catches the sun
As a rainbow trout passes by
Deep within the water of the river
Feeding quietly in the calm eddy
Just below the rapids.

Two beavers, swimming by
Dragging a large branch
As they build another dam,
A new home to raise their young.

A swallow, diving and dashing,
In and out of it's riverbank nest
Always searching for food
To feeds it's family.

Suddenly, on the path ahead of me
A garter snake silently slithers away
Into the long grass
And quickly disappears from sight.

On the corner where the two rivers
    meet
Near where the old settler's cabin
    once stood.
The grand and stately Blue Heron
Standing proudly and quietly,
Among the bullrushes at the river's
    edge
Silently guarding it's habitat, year
    after year.

A peaceful calm and joy
Transcends, surrounds and envelops
    me
As I watch nature unfold before my
    eyes.
As it's hidden gems appear for a
    moment.
Then, disappear back into their world.

No words need to be spoken
As I am left
In this solitude with my thoughts.
I silently continue my trek down the
    river.

For in this is a peaceful natural world,
One which has not been disrupted and
    disturbed,
One which provides a refuge and
    escape,
One which truly transcends and leaves
    behind
The trails and tribulations of life
    around me.

Allowing me to share in
And be a part of it
For a few brief relaxing minutes
Before I return
To my life in the outside world.
Or is this world actually the reality
Of what my life should be?

A Winter Walk

Like a thousand sharp knives
The bitter, biting and frigid wind
Cuts through me as I walk along.
My eyes watering in the luminous
    brightness,
The droplets, instantly freezing,
As they descend to my cheeks.

Within minutes, I cannot feel
My fingers or my toes.
My entire body is shaking
To fight the glacial conditions
Yet I walk on.

Moving quickly through
This incredibly beautiful frozen
    landscape.
A hazy mist rising off the river
Coating the trees and the bushes
With a stunning wintery covering of
    frost.
Glistening in the bright winter sun.

Glowing icicles hanging,
Glimmering in the winter's sun
Sending reflections of rainbows
To the snowy ground below.

The wind creating
A spontaneous snow shower
As the frost is shaken from the
    branches.
Only to be instantly replaced
By the rising polar mist rising from
    the river.

A brilliant, shimmering sun
Shines down on the sparkling snow,
Blinding me as I move along
With the dazzling bright reflection
In my eyes from the frozen ground.

There is an eerie surrounding silence,
Except for me, nothing is moving
In these chilling arctic conditions.
Yet there is a natural beauty to be
    found
In even these, the harshest of
    conditions.

Generating an inner warmth of
    contentment
To contrast with the raw, chilling
    exterior.
This climatic atmosphere combines
To create the challenge and the magic
Of another winter wonderland walk
On this crisp, cold and blustery
    morning.

Lights in the Night

Walking through the dimly lit park
With a happy, bounding dog by my
    side
Who is continually sniffing and
    exploring
All the new scents around him.

As I enjoy the cool autumn evening
    air,
I look out across the shadowy river
At a million sparking lights
Shining brightly,
Contrasting and conflicting
With the deep darkness of the night.

They are not
The twinkling lights of celestial
    bodies
High in the heavens above me.
There are many different hues,
Some steady, others flickering,
Some bright, others muted.
All from the ground sending
An incandescent glow high
Into the sable sky above.

The lights, I am observing,
Are always sparkling, shimmering
    and shining.
Their radiant luminescence,
Coming together as one to reach out
Into the pitch-black darkness.

They create a warm inner glow
Deep within my soul,
Knowing they are the lights
Of millions of other souls
Just like mine
Living their lives, day to day.

Stopping and standing motionless
For a moment to quietly watch.
I gaze across the dark river
With a sense of enchantment and
    fascination,
Spellbound, hypnotized and
    mesmerized
By the brilliant lights of New York
    City.

Before Dawn

Walking along,
The black darkness
Surrounds and envelops me.
With only a few small ground lights
Leading me along the path.

There are no distinct shapes
On the ground or in the sky.
Nothing can be seen.
Nothing but the sinister shadows
Of an indistinct, inky blackness
As I move forward
Enjoying the silence,
The serenity, the solitude
The stillness of early morning.

Slowly, ever so slowly
The clouds high above me
Take on a deep crimson glow
As dark shadows emerge
From the depths
Of my ebony surroundings.
Grey ghostly shapes
Spring to life all around me
With the clouds, now glowing
A bright phosphorus red.

Still nothing in nature stirs
As the world shifts
From the deep darkness
Taking on a charcoal grey appearance.
The world has not yet awakened
As the morning sky comes alive
With an ever-brighter predawn glow
Of scarlet red, tangerine orange and
    citrus yellow
Dancing on the fringes of the eastern
    horizon.

Forecasting, forewarning, foretelling
Of the daybreak soon to follow
As a new day will begin
And the world will spring to life
From it's deep slumber of the night.

Sharing the Spirit of the Season

Sometimes one has to stop
In the middle of the road
To gaze upon a beautiful sight.
A thousand twinkling lights
Sending a fluorescent beacon,
A brilliant brightness,
High into the dark night sky.

This breathtaking seasonal display
Astounds anyone who takes the time
To look and watch in wonder.
A peaceful serenity,
A sense of serendipity
Descends and envelops the scene.

The snow, glowing brightly
With reflecting colours
Ever-changing, moment to moment,
From a phenomenal purple
To a marvellous red
To a magnificent green
To a majestic yellow.

In the window of the home
A cheerful photogenic Santa
Greets everyone with a warm wave
As a happy snowman
And other magical winter scenes
Adorn and light up the walls,
Filling the night sky with a delightful
    glow.

So many Christmas trees
Lined up in formation,
Seasonal soldiers filling the snowy
    yard
With a rainbow of beaming colours.
Several strands of lights reaching up
Into the darkness
Spreading the joy of the season.

A flag waving gently in the wind
Taking on the various shades
Of the changing colourful glow
    encircling it.
In this jaded world of ours,
Someone took the time
To bring a sense of wonder and joy
To strangers who pass their home.

During this special time of the year,
Quietly looking at this display,
One comes to understand
The true sense of what
This season is all about.

For when one person
Can bring happiness
To so many others
By simply sharing
Their love of the season.
All the while hoping this warm
    feeling
Will be experienced by everyone
Throughout the entire year.

Demonstrating to all
Who pass this wondrous home
That one person can truly
Change the world around them.
Giving back to their fellow man
Without expecting anything in return.
Touching and affecting people
They don't even know.
One person passing to so many others
The true spirit of the Season.

A Quiet Contentment

Sitting quietly outside
With my best furry friend
We are free at last,
Having escaped the frozen tundra of
    home.
Listening to the gentle, echoing
    cooing
Of a morning dove.
A cool, tranquil early morning breeze
Blowing the humidity away
From the night before.

Every once in a while
My puppy lifts his head
Growling softly
At a passing person, dog, or squirrel.
Then, dropping down
Returning to his peaceful slumber.

The sun, having risen
Just a short time ago
Rising slowly over the edge of our
    building
Sending warm rays to all below,
Another beautiful day is beginning.

As I look around
Through bleary, sleep-filled eyes
I see a flag waving gently in the wind
Shimmering and rippling, covered
    with dew,
Reflecting the ever-increasing
    sunlight.
The palm trees around me, swaying
    gently
Hypnotizing in their dance of the
    dawn.

Overhead, a flock of bright green
    parrots
Fly quickly by, noisily squawking
As they disappear from sight.
Their clamour still echoing in the sky
Long after they have vanished from
    view.

Grey, fluffy clouds
Gathering on the distant horizon,
Slowly moving towards me
Forewarning, foretelling, forecasting
A harbinger promising a future storm.

My puppy still blissfully sleeping by
    my side
As I sip my morning cup of Earl Grey
    tea,
Quietly watching the awakening
    world around me
Content, happy, and gratified
To peacefully welcome another day in
    my life.

The Walk

**Dedicated to the Never Alone
Cancer Foundation**

Hundreds of legs,
Canine and human,
So many paws
Walked for a great cause
Under a canopy of green.
Moving together as one.

The sounds of excited
Barking and chatter
Echoed through the trees
And filled the air
As the line of people and pets,
So many different sizes and breeds
Walked through the park.

Each step taken
Raised more money to help
Fight the war
Too many are waging.
Each cancer warrior
Doing what needs to be done.

So many walking
For loved ones lost.
Remembering them fondly
With pins, stickers and signs
On a warm autumn day
Living, loving and laughing
As we walked along the path
Overlooking muddy brown waters of
    the river.

As the seemingly never-ending
Line of people and pets
Moved through the park
The sun shining down
Warming all the hearts and souls
With so much love being shared
Between the humans and their
    puppies
As we moved forward.

It was one of those moments
In our lives
We will always remember.
It will remain
In our memories and our hearts
As the special day
We walked with our furry friends

To support
Cancer warriors and their families,
To fight back
Against this dreaded disease,
To honour
Those who fight the battle day after
    day,
To fondly remember
Those who are no longer with us,
To walk and share time
With so many others
Who share a common bond.

The Kaleidoscope of Society

**Dedicated to the Winnipeg Fringe
Festival**

Sitting quietly alone in the Square
After the morning storm has passed,
Sipping my cafe mocha.
Trying desperately
To raise my energy levels,
To get my blood flowing
With another show to perform.

Soft melodic strains
Of a folk singer
Interrupted from time to time
By the sounds of sirens rushing by.
I look around me,
Watching toes tapping
In time to the music.

A chalk painter
Skillfully decorating the walkway.
So many different characters
Wander in on this quiet morning.
A gentle rain is now falling
Helping to keep the day cool.

Dogs of all shapes and sizes
Taking their humans for a walk.
Two young lovers pass by
Totally oblivious to the world
Around them,
Completely and fully focussed
On each other.

The sound of children's laughter,
Playing games,
Living such a simple life.
The smells
Of a wonderful assortment of food
Fills the air from the food trucks
Lining the square.

The world is full of hugs, once again,
As friends greet friends
During these days
Of the celebration of theatre.
As the Square fills,
The noise level grows
And the quiet solitude
Of the morning slips away.
It is the sound of happy chatter
As another day begins.

My cafe mocha is gone.
The time has come for me
To return to the theatre,
To the stage I love so much.
Walking slowly,
Basking in the warmth of the midday
    sun.

Then, quickly disappearing
Into the darkness of the theatre.
Waiting for the audience to arrive
With eager anticipation,
Having experienced
The kaleidoscope of society,
I am ready to begin,
To prepare for the show ahead.

Walking in the Rain

There is a steady bone-chilling rain
    falling.
The sky, a unbroken carpet of dull and
    dark grey.
Heavy droplets falling continually on
    our heads
From the branches overhead.
The ground is completely soaked,
My feet, getting wetter and colder
With each forlorn step we take.

There is no shelter from the downpour.
But we must muster on,
Waiting for the dog
To complete what he needs to do
Before we can take shelter
From the storm.

As much as I dislike
The inhospitable weather,
He absolutely loves it,
Enjoying every single moment.
As much as I shiver uncontrollably in
    the wind,
He relishes the coolness surrounding
    us.
He would walk all day in these
    elements
Without hesitation, if allowed to do so.

As the rain increases
From a drizzle to a steady downpour.
The frosty wind picks up,
Turning more frigid with each passing
    minute
Adding further
To my complete discomfort and
    distain.

The more I want to go inside,
The more he wants to walk
Leading me further from home.
Both of us,
Completely soaked from head to paw,
But still we stroll on.

As the rain grows even heavier,
The wind grows even stronger,
The sky grows even darker
All of which complements
My ever-increasing gloomy mood
To be outside on such a day.

As I slowly trudge, step by step,
Being pulled forward,
Further and further from the direction
I would like to be headed
By an ever more excited canine
Enjoying, sniffing and exploring
Each soaked blade of grass
And each dripping bush.

Suddenly, he stops
Dead in his tracks
And circles quickly around.
Is it time?
Will it finally happen?
Will we be able to head home?

Now, at last,
I am happily leading the way
As our chilly and saturated walk
Will soon quickly come to an end.
The time has finally arrived
For a warm blanket
And a hot cup of tea
With the happy and contented dog,
Snuggled, sleeping serenely
By my side under the covers.

Section 8
Music and Sports

The Last Exit

As he steps off the mound
One last time
His arm is sore,
His mind is tired,
His body is worn out.
It is telling him
The time has finally come.

All of his fans
Cheer loudly for him
Waving at him with love.
He tips his cap to them
As he thinks back
To the first time
He walked onto the field
So many years ago.
So young, so excited,
So filled with the dream
Of what was to come.

Then, after a long, slow walk
He enters the dugout
One last time.
His team enthusiastically greets him
With hugs, affection and respect.
They all know
The meaning of his last walk off the
    field,
His final exit from the game.

As he sits quietly in the corner,
A tear comes to his eye,
Another moment of reflection
Remembering all he has accomplished
Over his many years playing the
    game.

His life will continue
He will move on to a new chapter
But he will no longer
Be a part of the game
He loves so much.
The game that has been his life
For all of his life.

He watches in mute silence
As the game continues
Realizing the game is much more
Than just one person
It will carry on without him.
But he will be fondly remembered
As a part of his team's history.

For the mark
He has made on the game
Will last forever,
Never to be forgotten.
Sitting alone in his corner,
He quietly reflects on his past
Enjoying his last moments
In the dugout with his team.
Filled with the hope
Of a changed yet bright new future.

The Season is Over!

The season is over!
The final game has been played
No championship parade will be held
For the team has lost their final game.
The uniforms and utensils of the game
Have been put away for one last time,

The players will all head home
Some never to return.
Year after year,
The team is never exactly the same.
The close camaraderie felt this year
Will not be repeated
But will have to be recreated
As changes will be made.

The stadium,
Once filled with a loud and adoring
    crowd
Will sit silent until next season.
No more burgers or beer will be sold.
The fans will put away
Their bells and horns,
Their caps and jerseys.
No more faces will be painted,
No more tailgates will be held.

They will sit quietly at home
Watching another city celebrate
As another team wins the
    championship.
They came so close
But that does not matter now.
Their team did not win!

So, for now, they will be forced to
    wait
Until another season begins next year.
The team, once again,
Will put on their uniform,

Old players will return,
New players will join them.
A new spirit, a new camaraderie will
    emerge
As they begin a new journey.

The new season will start
With the hope of finally winning
The golden grail,
The championship of their sport.
The stadium will be filled with fans
All wearing their colours,
All cheering with the same wild
    enthusiasm

Year after year.
A new hope,
A new dream,
A new flame of desire
Will be ignited.
Will this be the year to celebrate
Or like other years to commiserate
And forced to wait once again?

In the end,
There will only be one team
Who will call themselves
The Champions.
But for the players
And the fans alike
The love of the game,
The desire to win,
The hope of the elusive championship
Will all spring to life, once again.

The Olympic Spirit

Every four years
The youth of the world
Comes together
With excitement and enthusiasm
For the sporting adventures
Ahead of them.

The flame of togetherness and
    reconciliation
Is lit and burns brightly
For just a few short days.
The world watches
With an expectancy and anticipation
Allowing ourselves to escape
The turmoil and the troubled times
We have all been living through

As the youth compete
With by a common bond of
Fellowship and friendship.
We all experience
The excellence of youth
At it's very best
On display for all to watch.

Then, suddenly,
In far too short a time
It is over
As everyone gathers
One last time
Before returning home
To all corners of our
Blue and green planet.

There is a moment
Of reflection and sadness
As the flame is extinguished
Mingled with a renewed sense of
    hope
Knowing in four years
It will be relit
And, once again,
The world will come together

The call is sent out
To the children of the world
To gather in the spirit of sport
Four years hence.

One is left
With fond memories
Of the excellence
We have witnessed
Yet wondering
What today will bring
Combined with the sense of hope
For the future.

The Olympic Spirit
Will remain alive and strong
As the world is left
With a feeling of fulfillment,
Having closely watched
Their amazing accomplishments.
While looking forward to the next
    time
The world will gather together!

The Music of our Lives

Music is, has been,
And will always be
A guiding force in our lives.
Something for us
To treasure and enjoy
As we walk along
The path through life.

When we feel pressure,
It relaxes us.
When we feel sad,
It delights us with joy.
When we feel lonely,
It carries us closer to others.
When we feel a sense of apathy,
It enthrals and inspires us.

From concerts to opera,
From ballet to musical theatre,
From symphony to singers.
It entertains us though difficult times,
It brings us together, out of isolation,
It uplifts our spirits,
It motivates us into action.

It is heard
In the beautiful harmonies of a choir
In the lovely melodies of a quartet,
In the energy and strength of a
    symphony.
In the simple, sweet solo voice of a
    child
As they laugh and sing out with joy,
Without fear, without recrimination.

Music is all around us
We just need to listen
And we will hear it.
It is in the wind
As it rustles though
The leaves on the trees.

It is in the many songbirds
We hear as we stroll though nature.
It is in the haunting cry
Of the wolf and the loon
Heard so distinctly in the wilderness.
It is in the friendly bark of a dog
Wanting to run and play.

Music enhances everything,
Making our world a better place,
Creating a balanced synergy allowing
    us
To live more joyful, contented days.
It gives us a sense
Of inner harmony and happiness
Empowering us to live more fulfilled
    lives.

Sports Fans are Strange

Sports fans are strange.
Over the years,
They live and die
With their teams.
How good their day will be
Very often depends on whether
Their team wins or loses.
Day by day, week by week,
The happiness in the lives
Will be determined
By how well their team is doing.

Then,
When the season comes to an end
More often than not
With a heart-breaking loss,
They feel their life
As they know it
Has come to an end.

Yet, by the next morning
They are already thinking about
And waiting for the next season.
There is always hope
That next year will be the year
Their team wins it all!

The seed of excitement is planted
As they move on
Refusing to believe
Or even consider
That their chosen team is not
The very best in their sport.
So, sports fans will always
Be ready to wait and see and cheer,
As, once again, another season
Will begin sometime next year.

For in the mind of the sports fan
There is always hope for the future.
The disappointment of the present
Will be quickly put aside.
The past is forgotten long ago.
Yes, sports fans are strange.
Perhaps, at the same time,
We can all learn from them.

The Youth of our World

And so it begins once again!
The youth of our world
Gathering together in competition
As they have for hundreds of years.
Occasionally, in our own country
But, more often, halfway around the
    world.

In a distant land
Where their day is our night
When the sun is up over there,
We see the moon.
As they compete,
We will be asleep
For when we are awake,
They will be in deep slumber.

But wherever the gathering takes
    place
We will watch with eager anticipation
At all times of the day and night.
As they come together in celebration,
In competition, in peace.

As it all commences,
They will be proudly
Waving their country's flag,
Walking together, as a group
With uniforms to match.
We watch an array of colours
As they enter the stadium.

Flag-bearer's proudly leading their
    team,
Flying their country's flag
Red and white,
Red, white and blue,
Gold and blue,
Orange, white and green,

Black, red and yellow,
A variety of coloured crosses, circles
    and shapes

All proudly march into the stadium
Together, as a team, as a country
Waving with heartwarming happiness
To their families,
To their friends,
To their homeland.

Letting everyone know
They will try their very best
To make those watching proud
To be Canadian, to be American,
To be a citizen of the country they
    represent,
Be it large or be it small.

The smiles on their faces
Warm the hearts
Of everyone around the world.
The deep, dark divisions
Of a troubled planet in turmoil
Will be put aside for two short weeks
As the best of our youth
Skillfully engage one another
For supremacy in their chosen sport.

For one brief moment in time,
Sports will supersede politics,
Unification will outshine divisiveness,
The equipment of competition
Will replace the weapons of war.
The love of sport and mutual respect
Will supplant deep-seeded contempt.

For the next fortnight,
As we bear witness
To the goodwill of competition
And the spectacle of sports
As it unfolds before us.

We need to not only observe
But to follow the example
Shown by the youth of our world.
For they will be the ones
Who will lead us into the future.

The Roller Coaster of Emotion

Just a small slip
On the ice or in the snow
Disrupts and destroys the dream.
A momentary look of disbelief
Followed by a vacant emotional stare
Into the distance.
The deep-seeded feeling
Of being alone in the world,
Having let so many people down.
Their family, their team, their country
All crying tears of support for them.

Slowly rising
From the heavy weight of defeat,
The feeling of complete desolation,
The lingering loneliness of loss.
Unsure how to pick up the pieces,
To start again,
To continue the journey
To fulfill the dream of a lifetime.

Then, there are those who feel
The achievement, the euphoria,
The attainment of the goal and the
    dream
The same moment of disbelief
As tears of joy begin to flow.
Knowing they have found
The ultimate success
At the top of their sport.

Their family, their team, their county
Erupts with happiness and jubilation
As a new hero is crowned.
All the years of commitment,
The dedication and the hard work
Have culminated in reaching
The pinnacle of success
During this perfect moment in their
    lives.

Sometimes, we watch
In muted disbelief and silence
Then, at other times,
With loud and boisterous noise
At the success and the failure,
At the happiness and the sadness,
At the joy and the desolation
Riding the roller coaster of emotion
Of all the athletes in competition.

We feel an empathy with them
Both in their celebration
And in their dejection.
For world is watching
As the events continually unfold.
The endeavour, the effort, the
    exertion,
The moments of delight and despair.
Shared by all every four years
As the history of another Olympic
    Games
Manifests, proclaims and reveals itself
    to us.

The Joy of Resound

Sensational, sweet sopranos
Amazing, alluring altos
Tremendous, transporting tenors
Beautiful, blissful baritones and
    basses
All led by a musical genius
Who epitomizes the joy of music.

Perfect harmonies
Carried on the wings of the wind.
Echoing through the cloisters
Reaching into the heavens.
Leaving the listeners,
Mesmerized and transfixed,
As each musical piece
Come to an end
And another begins.

The sun shining
Through the stained glass windows
Adds to the magic of the moment.
Each note
Uplifting the spirit,
Cleansing the soul.
Each voice
Singing with happy passion.
All voices coming together
As one voice.

The regal, relaxing sound
Of an organ
Merging with
The eerie, haunting melody
Of an oboe.
Bach with the Beatles,
The Scriptures with Simon and
    Garfunkel
All fused together.

So different and diversified
Yet working as one
To bring a moment of tranquility,
A moment of hope,
A moment of peace
In the turmoil of our troubled world.

All the sights and sounds
Blending so beautifully together.
The music and the harmonies
Continue to echo in our minds
Long after the concert has ended.

Just Like That!

**Dedicated to all the sports fans
who support teams of unfulfilled
glory**

Just like that
It is over!
No warning, no tomorrow,
No more games
So much regret,
So many tears
Just a feeling of despair and anger.

So much potential
Crushed by the weight of defeat,
Gone forever.
Put quite simply,
It is over yet incomplete
For the season is done.

All the hopes
Of the team,
All the dreams
Of their fans
Lost forever,
Dashed in one moment of time.

Changes will be made
Some will retire,
Some will move on,
Some will join,
But it will never be the same
For this team.

This was to be
Their time of glory,
Their moment of destiny
Making their mark in history.

Instead, there is
The bitter taste of defeat.
A defeat, so unexpected,
One that should never have happened,
One that will not be forgotten or
    forgiven
For a long time.

All that is left,
Now and forever,
The desperate, empty feeling
Of missed opportunity,
Of unkept promises,
Of unfulfilled glory.

From elation and joy
To dejection and sadness
On the bench and in the stands.
In such a short period of time
For just like that
It is over!

Section 9
Biking

A Smoky Ride

Written by Laurie Fischer

As soon as anyone ventures
From the safety of their home
They are immediately surrounded
By a hazy mist
Covering the outside world.

The sun has become
A red smouldering fireball high
    above,
Dashing in and out
Of the smoky clouds
Completely obscuring the opaque sky

As I ride
My breathing is strained,
Coughing and wheezing,
My chest aches,
My throat burns,
My nose fills
With the intense smouldering scent.
My eyes sting
In the thick musty air.

Yet I know I must ride on.
For so many children
Depend on my efforts
As I ride deep
Into the grey vapour
Of this murky world.

The trees surround me,
Shrouded, almost indistinguishable,
Eerie forms, camouflaged and
    concealed.
All of nature is hidden away
As the arid fog extends everywhere
With the smell of burned wood.

There is no escape
For anyone or anything
From the foreboding curtain of smog.
Peddling hard,
I carry on, pushing forward,
Straining, stressing and struggling
With a renewed sense of urgency
To reach the end of my journey

So I can escape inside
Away from this eerie and strange
    world.
Knowing tomorrow,
I will venture forth, once again,
Fighting these mysterious elements
To help all the children
Who are battling for their lives.

Riding In The Heat Of Summer

The sun shines brightly
Through the canopy of trees
Creating dancing shadows
On the ground as I ride by
Feeling the surging heat
Rising from the asphalt.

The searing summery wind
Creates a symphony of sound
As it passes
Through the branches
Pushing me along the pathway.

Animals of all shapes and sizes
Quietly basking in the shade,
Lethargic in the sultriness
Of another summer day,
Too lazy to wander very far.

I hear but can not see
Birds all around me
Singing brightly
Hidden from the stifling heat
In the branches of the trees.

Although the closeness
Of the muggy air surrounding me
Creates an ever-increasing burden
As I ride along.
The humidity oppressively
Bearing down on my energy.

Still I continue on
Despite the intense wall of warmth
Enjoying the sights and sounds
Of the summer swelter.
Wiping any wetness from my
    forehead
Before it descends
To blur my vision of the road ahead.

Deliberately increasing my speed
To create a self-propelling breeze
To cool myself as I surge forward
Towards the end of my journey.
Having, once again,
Conquered the oppressive elements
Of another summer heatwave.

This Beautiful Day!

It's a beautiful day.
The sun is shining brightly
Sharing it's wonderful warmth.
There's a pleasant breeze blowing
Welcoming us to the new day ahead.

The trees,
Covered in luscious green,
The flowers,
Blooming in a rainbow of colours
The birds flying by,
Singing cheerfully
To the world around them.

People starting to gather
Sharing the day with each other
After so many months of isolation.
Waving and calling out to one
    another,
At long last the world seems
To be coming together.

There's a wonderful positive vibe
As I cycle through this new world.
An optimistic, hopeful feeling,
An undeniable, upbeat sense of calm,
An unquestionable, promising
    sentiment
All of which have been absent for far
    too long.

Suddenly, the future looks as bright
As we all hoped it would
Even during our darkest hours.
We will never forget
What we have been though

But, now at last,
We are ready
To move forward together
To fight back against
That which has held us down
For so very long,
Ready to face whatever
The future will bring us,

Knowing we will be able
To overcome any obstacles
And to grow
With the opportunities ahead.
All those things
We have been impatiently waiting for
Are, once again, reawakening,
Returning to us
On this beautiful day!

Why I Do It

Why do I ride
Hour after hour,
Day after day,
Kilometre after kilometre?

I do it to fight
This insidious relentless disease
Hidden deep within my body,
Always waiting to attack.

I do it on behalf
Of all the children
Who face this monster
Each and every day.

I do it to support
All the families and friends
Of those children
Who watch, support and pray
For their little loved ones.

I do it with hope in my heart
That one day
All those who have
This unforgiving disease
Will win their battles.

I do it in loving memory
Of all those who have
Lost their fight
And for those who loved them,
Always remembering
And holding then close
In their hearts forever.

Why do I ask
So many others
For their help
To join me in this quest
As I ride on?

I do it
Because I can not
Do it alone.
I need all of their support
To join me
To kick cancer's butt and
To fight against kids' cancer.

So, I will continue to ride
To fight my own battle
And on behalf of those
Who can not do it for themselves.
Hour after hour,
Day after day,
Kilometre after kilometre.

The Joy of Riding

The sun shines down
Warming the wind
As the golden leaves
Fall from their high perches
And shower me as I ride along.

A familiar feeling of freedom
Descends, envelopes and covers me
Like a cozy warm blanket
On a cold December night.

A sense of serendipity surrounds me
As I glide through the early morning
    mist.
All the troubles of the world and my
    life
Quickly fade away
As a new adventure begins.

Nature reveals herself to me
As I progress
Deeper into her domain.
I become part of and disappear
Into her loving embrace
Looking around at her beauty.

With my favorite music
Playing in my ears,
Helping to propel me forward.
A sensation of complete happiness,
An awareness of absolute tranquility
Transcends upon me,
Carrying me along.

I am alone
But not lonely
For I am at peace with myself.
My thoughts are my own.
I ride at my own pace
Without any concerns or pressures.

With none of life's roadblocks
Holding me back.
I move quickly
With a sense of purpose
Entirely of my own making.

Enjoying every moment of
This quiet solitude,
This relaxing escape,
Alone with nature,
At one with myself
And the world around me.
All this and so much more is
The joy of riding.

Into the Culvert

Such an incredibly beautiful day for
   a ride
With just more lap and then
   homeward bound.
When, without any warning,
My front wheel slips off the road
And disappears into the culvert.
The bike abruptly stops
But momentum continues
To carry me forward

From that moment on
My world moves
In slow surreal motion.
There is absolutely
No time to think
About how this will end.
No time to react
To uncontrollable events
Now confronting me.
No time to change
What is about to happen.
No time for fear
As I feel my entire body
Launched into the air
Over my handle bars.

I land heavily on the cement pad
My chest hitting first,
Taking the full brunt.
My arms, following at awkward
   angles,
Ending with a sudden and complete
   stop.
My head hitting the ground,
Momentarily dazing me.
Immediate and intense pain
Across my chest,
Spreading down both arms.

Realizing in my stunned stupor
That I am still alive.
I must be
As the strange pain escalates
Through my body.
My head aches from the impact,
But I can feel no blood
As my helmet saved me.

Trying to steady my breathing
And control the extreme discomfort
Emanating from my chest.
Both my legs are trapped
Inside the handlebars.
I know I must get them out
But, at this moment,
Easier said than done.
Finally able to extract myself,
Lying on the ground
Wondering if I will be able
To ride or even walk again.

From my prone position,
I gaze up at the beautiful blue sky
Stunned by all that has just occurred.
Remembering only moments ago
I was enjoying
The beauty of another ride
On a warm, sunny autumn morning.
Slowly standing,
Moving around, ever so cautiously.
At least knowing now,
I am able to walk

My bike lies totally helpless,
Like a wounded animal
Resting still in the culvert.
Realizing with sadness,
My riding has come to an end
For the foreseeable future

As the pain spreads
Throughout my body.
Nothing feels broken,
While all the muscles
In my chest, my arms and my legs
Tightening with each passing
    moment.

Slowly, ever so slowly,
I hobble away
Sadly knowing,
It will take time to recover
Before I can ride again.
Knowing one day,
I will be back
But when?

The Serenity and Serendipity of Cycling

My mind relaxes
Putting aside
All the troubles of my life.
My body energized
The aches and pains of
Age and disease forgotten.
A feeling of serenity
Surges through me
A sense of serendipity
Surrounds me.

Moving through the world
As the sun shines down,
As a gentle breeze
Blows me along,
As nature unfolds
Her beauty before me.

For just a few brief minutes
The turmoils of the world
Are forgotten.
A warm, peaceful feeling
Transcends upon and surges
Through my body,
As a blanket
Of passion and energy
Envelopes me.

All my senses are invigorated
For this moment,
My life is completely
Calm, composed and conciliated.
I am truly at peace
With myself and all around me
For this is
The serenity and serendipity of
  cycling.

Section 10
Our Puppies

My Constant Companion

His dark brown eyes
Gaze fondly up at me.
Asking nothing more
Than to be loved,
While always loving me
    unconditionally.

Filling my life with empathy
For when I am unhappy or unwell
He sits closer than ever
To share in my sadness.

Staying by my side
Throughout the storms of my life.
Never wandering far away from me.
Always sensing when I need him
    most.

Enjoying all the simple things in life.
Be it a walk, a treat or a belly rub.
Curling up quietly in my lap
Or sleeping closely beside me at night

Content to just be with me.
Always keeping a watchful eye,
Protecting me
From the woes of the world.

When others desert me
He is never far away.
Happy to always be
A part of my life.

I know all too well
One day he will no longer be here
But his memory will linger
With me for the rest of my life.

For when he goes,
He will take a part of me with him.
I will never be the same
Without him.

But I will be a better person
For having had the short time
We shared together in my life,
Just me and my constant companion.

Walking my Puppy

When walking my puppy
I am at peace with the world
As the beauty of nature
Surrounds us.
He is absolutely determined
To explore everything
That the world has to offer.
His excitement shown
In his speedy gait
As this is truly
His favourite time of the day.

There is no such thing
As a straight line.
Every movement,
Perceived or real,
Every smell, good, bad or ugly,
All of it is there to be
Sniffed out,
Fully uncovered and explored.

Everything around us
Is his and his alone.
We move forward
As quickly or as slowly
As he deems necessary.
With so many pit stops
Along the way.
I have time to reflect,
To use my imagination
To uncover new words and phrases
For my next poem.
Often jarred from my thoughts
By the anxious tug on the leash.

With yet another change of direction,
Always moving quickly
With excitement and anticipation

As he runs to uncover another
    mystery.
Only pausing momentarily
To mark the world as his own
Covering another dogs well-placed
    scent.
Then, moving on
To find a new adventure.

Every once in a while,
A sudden jarring halts our momentum
As we meet and greet
Another puppy and their human
Taking their own walk.
After much sniffing and greeting,
We move on.

For walking my puppy
Is a series of continuous,
Never-ending experiences
As we escape from everyday life.
Allowing him to his world of nature
As I am left
Within my world of imagination.
Together, enjoying
Each other's company
During this peaceful time together.

When and only when
He is ready
We return home.
After a quick drink
To replenish himself,
He curls up close beside me
In my most comfortable chair
As together we fall
Into a peaceful, well deserved
    slumber.

Who Has Rescued Whom?

I often wonder
When sharing our lives
With rescue pets
Who has really rescued whom?

For all the unconditional love,
Dedication and joy
We humans receive
From these special animals.
Are we rescuing them
Or are we being rescued?

When life settles down
And a new family member
Becomes a part of our life,
Over time, the connection
And the loving relationship
Grows ever stronger.

As we get to know
And fully appreciate
This new member of our clan
As they get to know,
To trust and to love us,
An unbreakable bond is created.
From the beginning,
We are happy to give them
The life they truly deserve.
No matter how it started
They have found
Their forever home.

But, in return,
We will discover
An unconditional love
Unlike any other
We have ever experienced
That will continue to grow
As time passes by.

Our lives are forever changed
By our fur-babies.
So, as much as we may believe
We have rescued them,
In reality, they have rescued us.
For they will always give us
So much more
Than we can ever give them.

Changing our lives for the better,
As the complications,
The turmoil and the troubles
Surrounding our lives
Becomes less important,
Almost inconsequential.

We feel an increasing inner peace,
An ongoing outward tranquility,
A sense of serene serendipity
Day after day,
Month after month,
Year after year.
So, the question remains
Who has rescued whom?

A Walk in the Dark

Darkness surround us
As an exited puppy
Runs across the damp dewy grass
To begin a nocturnal walk.

Flickering street lamps cast
Our dark moving images
Onto the ground.
The trees, hidden in the dark
Gently dance in the warm night
    breeze.
Their shadows mingle with ours
As we pass by.
There is not a sound
Except for the wind
Gently rustling the leaves above us.

The puppy has no interest
In the beauty of the night
Surrounding us.
As he runs from one new smell
To another, barely stopping
To do his business,
The reason we are out tonight.

A million stars, twinkling brightly,
In jet black sky.
The worlds beyond ours
Clearly visible as we walk along.
In wonderment, I watch
This beautiful extra-terrestrial display.
Thinking to myself
How small our troubled world really
    is
In the great expanse of space.
As important as we think we are,
We are but a tiny speck in the
    Universe.
There are so many more questions
Than answers to be found in the night
    sky.

Tugging anxiously on the leash,
Slightly afraid of the increasing
    shadows around him,
The puppy brings me back
To the reality of my present situation.
He has grown tired of exploring and
    marking.
The time has come to return
To the warmth of our home,
Yet another nocturnal walk
    completed.

Another Willy Wonka Day Begins

Each morning,
Running out of the darkness
Of our bedroom
A flash of brown and white,
Heading straight to the front door.

So enthusiastic,
So eager,
So energized
So ready to greet the world.
Overjoyed and thrilled
To be alive,
To be loved,
To live another day.

Extremely excited
To go for a morning walk
With his tail wildly wagging,
To sniff out so many new delights
The world outside has to offer.

Then, to return home
And energetically eat his breakfast
As if he has never been fed before.
Always pausing midway through
Waiting be lifted up
For a morning cuddle.

Forever full of early morning kisses,
To share with me
Whether or not, I am ready.
It matters little to him
For this is the fondness and friendship
He did not enjoy early in his life.

But now,
Completely content in his new world,
Happy to share
His unbridled devotion,
His uncontrollable zest,
His unbounded joy.
Having grown from
A sad, neglected, unwanted puppy
To this joyful, excitable, much loved
    dog.

Always ready to let everyone
Around him know
How he feels to
Wake up and greet
Each and every new day.

He has been freed from
Those early bonds of unhappiness
To live his life
In a world filled with love.

As much as we may give him,
He gives back
So much more to us.
And so it is
As another day begins
In the life of Willy Wonka.

Waiting to be Loved

I will never understand
For it is so far
Beyond my comprehension
Why anyone could or would
Neglect, abuse and abandon any
    animal.

Their trust is totally tainted,
Their devotion destroyed,
Their loyalty lost.
A shadow of what
They once were,
A silhouette of the potential
They could be.
A skeleton, a hollow shell
Completely broken, afraid, unloved.

So often,
They are simply cast aside,
Left without a home
Without a family,
Without any food to sustain them
Without any human to love
Completely abandoned and alone,
Left to fend for themselves
Against the cruel force of nature.

Only a precious few
Will be saved,
Will find a new home
Will discover the love of a human
Will recover the loyalty they lost
Will regain the trust taken from them.
They are quite simply
Waiting to be loved.

In return,
They will share with us
A lifetime of loyalty and devotion
A never-ending trust,
An uncompromising companionship.
An unconditional love
A relationship beyond which
Any human could possibly
Hope or wish to share.

Two Dogs

The fur-brothers are back together.
Even when separated
For a short period of time,
They are just not themselves
One always looking for the other.
Yet as with any reunion,
They greet each other
With unfathomable joy, enthusiasm
    and noise.

Like brothers,
From time to time, they will fight.
The younger,
Constantly in tease and attack mode.
The older,
Remaining patient for a limited time
Then, letting his brother know
When enough is enough.

So very different
In age, personality and demeanour
Yet complimenting each other
With a genuine brotherly love.
When together,
The older becoming more playful and
    youthful.
The younger growing more mature.
Both, so very different during our
    walks
Yet somehow knowing to
How to keep pace with one another.
For me, never fully knowing
Upon which side of me
Each will decide to walk,
Their leashes always seem to become
Inextricably tangled around my legs.

The younger,
Constantly stopping to explore.
The older,
Waiting patiently to continue the walk
Occasionally stopping to sniff
Until pushed aside by
The younger
Who never hesitates to pee
On his fur-brother's head
When they are too close together.

Then, covering him with dirt
As he kicks to mark his spot
With complete enthusiasm and
    delight.
The older,
Taking it all in stride,
Shaking off the dirt,
Ready to move on.

More often than not,
Each will walk
In completely different directions
Yet able, when they want
To walk perfectly in sync
Shoulder to shoulder.

Sleeping together,
Always such an adventure.
The younger not hesitating
To lie on his brother's head
With no respect for space and
    separation
Until with a warning growl the older
Moves away to claim his own new
    spot.

Always feeding off
Each other's loud barking
When someone or another dog
Dares to pass by.
The older one, leading the way
Always knowing exactly
What he is growling at.

The younger one,
Having absolutely no idea
Exactly what is happening
But joining with his high pitched
    howl
Simply because his fur-brother is
    barking.
Just happy to add his own sounds
To the noisy symphony filling our
    ears.

Anyone who has two dogs in their
    lives
Will fully understand our experiences.
Their daily escapades and adventures
May be somewhat different
But they share with empathy
The adventures and the happiness
Of living with and loving two dogs.

Our Fur Babies

Hug and love your fur babies
For you never know
When they will be gone forever.
Each and every day we hear about
Another one crossing
Over the Rainbow Bridge.

Gone forever but always
Living on in our hearts.
They love us unconditionally,
Their love surpassing any other
We will have during our time,
Throughout our journey.

Complementing and completing our
    lives
With their constant close
    companionship.
Always by our side
Throughout their entire lives.
Needing us
As much as we need them,
Truly the perfect simpatico
    relationship.

Yet their lives
Are so much shorter than ours
Perhaps, because they give us
All they have to give
In their time with us.
Offering us
Their uncompromising, unending,
    undying love.

Always by our side
Sharing our tears, comforting us
Through the toughest of times
Celebrating with us,
Sharing our joy
Through the happiest of times.

We need to share
Our love with them.
For there is absolutely no doubt
They make our lives
So much better with them
Than they would be without them.

We must always
Take the time
To hug and to love
Our fur babies.
For we will miss them
So very much
When they are gone
And we never know
When the hug we give them
May be the last one.

Easier To Love

Dogs are so much
Easier to love than humans.
When wondering why
It is very simple to understand.

They are always ready
To play with each other
Whenever they meet.
Sniffing each other's behinds,
They create a bond of lifetime
    friendship.

Let's not forget all those humans.
Politicians and people in business
Who do exactly the same thing.
Not for a lifetime of friendship
But to ambitiously get ahead!

Dogs love
All the simple things in life
That humans so often ignore.
Walks, belly rubs
Or just a simple kind word
Gives them uncontrollable and
    complete joy.

When they walk with us,
They explore everything around them,
Sniffing and pawing,
Never wanting to miss anything,
Sharing the joy of just being alive.

No matter what happens in our lives
They are always beside us.
To lift us up
When we are sad,
To lie beside us
When we are not well,
To share our joy
When we are happy.

They will protect us
Without any hesitation, uncertainty or
    fear,
Always putting themselves
Between any danger, perceived or
    real,
And those they love.

Dogs possess an ability
To love unconditionally.
Even those who mistreat them,
Those who do not
Deserve their love.
They are loyal beyond belief
Even to those who do not
Deserve their loyalty.

They will never change
For their unconditional love and
    loyalty
Are inherent deep within their souls.
It sets them apart from humans
These are the reasons why
They are so much easier to love.

Willy Wonka Awakens

It's 5am.
It is still dark outside.
Hours before the sun will rise.
All I want to do it sleep.
All Willy wants to do is give me a
    bath.
So excited to greet the new day.
I will be too… but much later.

He misses nothing
As my body is attacked
By his sharp, nibbling teeth
By his loving, lightning-quick tongue,
Face, ears,
Hands, fingers,
Arms, legs, toes,
Anything within the reach
Of his teeth and tongue is fair game.

It is useless to put up a fight.
He will simply wait
Before starting all over again.
His eyes glowing with delight.
So happy to ensure
I start and share my day with him.

At long last, he tires
Stretching out full length beside me
Slumbering contently and quietly.
In my sleep-induced state
I ask myself
How long will it last?
Probably, not long
Before the next onslaught begins.

And, so, at his request,
More like his demand
My day begins before the sun rises.
It is a small price to pay
For such love and devotion
Making my life richer.
Well worth the fatigue
As I can always take a cat-nap
Or should I say dog-nap later.

Oh no, here he comes again!

The Unbreakable Bond

Dedicated to anyone who has lost their BFF (Best Furry Friend).

They were always your best friend.
The bond between you, unbreakable.
Even now and for the rest of your life,
It will continue
Deep within your heart.
For absence does not take away,
Destroy or diminish that special love.

Your time together,
Filled with countless fond memories,
Many adventures, much love.
Always the best companion,
Committed to each other,
Consoling or celebrating.
Simply being there for each other.

Two characters,
So different in nature
With a bond so strong
Sharing a lifetime together,
One always seeming to know
What the other needed
Exactly when they needed it.

Life will go on
But will never be the same
For you have been left
With an cold hole in your heart.
Yet time will help to heal
With all the warm memories
You will always hold so close and so
    dear.

Your time together,
So much shorter
Than either of you would have liked
But it will be the time you had
Not the time lost,
Now forever gone,
You will always remember.

My Best Pal

He's my best pal.
We go together like bread and butter.
We are two sides of the same coin.
He understands me better
Than anyone else in my life.
Good times and bad times
We go through everything together.
And life is so much better
With him by my side.

Each of us needs a best pal.
Since, as humans, we are so different,
So are they.
Some are large, some are small.
Some are loud, some are quiet.
Some are dogs, some are cats,
Some are birds, some are reptiles.

Every kind of non-human
You can ever imagine
Will become best pals for us.
We need them more than
We will ever admit to ourselves.
Unlike people, they do not judge us.
They love us unconditionally,
They love us just as we are,
Asking so little in return.

Always there by our side,
Walking the path of life with us.
We know they will leave us
In far too short a time.
Yet while they are here
They make our lives complete.

They bring us joy
When we feel sadness.
They bring us love
When we feel alone.
They bring us light
When we feel darkness.
They bring us peace
When our lives are in turmoil.

Yes, he's my best pal.
We go together like bread and butter.
We are two sides of the same coin.
He understands me better
Than anyone else in my life.
Good times and bad times
We go through everything together
And life is so much better
With him by my side.

The Cost of Love

She sits in the park,
A lonely figure,
I see the shiny glint of a tear
Running down her cheek
In the bright sunshine.

Once so happy and content
Relaxing each day
Enjoying
The solitude and the sunshine
With her little fluffy companion.

Quietly greeting everyone
Who passed by
With a nod and a smile.
Her friendly puppy barking loudly
At anyone who ventured near them,

Now, she sits in the sun,
A lonely, solitary figure
For her fur-baby, without warning,
Crossed the rainbow bridge
Just a few days ago.

As I pass by
With my puppy
I want to stop and share.
Giving her a moment
Of the puppy love
She so desperately needs.

Yet, at the same time,
I do not want to assume or presume.
For it may do
More harm than good.
With the wounds of her heart
Being so fresh.

I will wait,
Giving her the time
She needs to grieve alone.
Knowing next time
She will be ready
For some love from another puppy.

I pass by
Smiling at her,
Sharing her sadness from a distance.
Having felt that same loss before,
Knowing I will feel it again one day.
For that is the cost
Of loving and being loved.

Sleep Well, My Little Boy

**Dedicated to our little boy, Willy
Wonka**

Usually watching the sunset
Brings me peace and contentment
But tonight
I feel an inner turmoil and sadness
Realizing this is the end
Of the first day of forever
Without him in our lives.

He brought us such happiness.
Some say we rescued him
But we know he rescued us.
It has often been said
Time heals all.
Well, it will take longer
Than I may have
For this pain to completely disappear.

Life was not fair for him.
Just as his life changed
For the better, it was ended
By the incredible inner wounds
Thrust upon him by uncaring people
When he was a puppy.

So, as I watch the sun
Dip below the horizon
I know he is resting peacefully
As memories of his short life
Overwhelm me with sadness.
Tomorrow I hope
They will start to bring
Solace to my broken heart

We know how lucky
We have been to share his life,
To make it so much better for him,
To bring him love and joy.
But as the day ends and darkness
    descends
It matches the mood of my soul,

I will think of him often,
Lovingly remembering
How good he was for us,
How good he was to us.

Sleep well and sleep in peace, my
    little boy
Knowing how loved you were.

Goodbye Willy! Hello Lilly!

Goodbye Willy!
So suddenly,
He crossed the Rainbow Bridge
Gone without warning.
Far too soon,
Far too young,
Never to be forgotten
A cloud of despair and sadness
Descended upon our home .
Seemingly no escape,
No reprieve from the shock.

Hello Lily!
Arrived to rescue us.
A tiny bundle of energy and love.
Replacing the gloom and storm clouds
That were enveloping our lives,
Lifting us back into the sunshine.
New, excited, different,
Not replacing our loss
But enhancing our lives.
So happy to have found
Her forever home.

Goodbye Willy!
Thank you for the years
You shared with us.
You will always be missed.
Never to be forgotten.
Fondly remembered forever!

Hello Lily!
Thank you for the happiness
You have brought back into our lives.
We may have rescued you
But you have saved us!
We are looking forward
To many years together!

Goodbye Willy!
Hello Lily!

Crossing the Rainbow Bridge

With his final breath
His long journey began.
He could hear
The misery and the cries
Of his loved ones
Growing ever fainter
As he walked further.
For now, at last,
He was free
From the pain and the suffering
He had felt for so long.

As he came to the Bridge
He sniffed around,
Searching for scents
That had once been
So familiar to him.
Finding none,
He moved on.

Halfway across,
He paused for a moment
Looking back, remembering,
Feeling the pull and the love
Of his humans.
The people who had
Cared for and loved him
Throughout the days of his life.

He knew instinctively
He had to keep moving
As slowly he edged forward.
The power that had once held him
Was quickly fading into his memory.
He would always remember
Those he had loved and had loved
    him
So strongly throughout his short life.

He instinctively sensed
He would see them again
Not knowing how or when
But knowing they would
Reunite with him.
Confidently, he moved on
Crossing the Rainbow Bridge
Into the unknown beyond.

He would wait,
Lovingly and patiently,
For however long it would take
For them to return to him
Sometime in the future.
He knew now what they did not,
That one day
They would be together again.

Section 11
Our Lives

Confrontation or Cooperation

Our lives seem
To be dictated by confrontation
Fuelled by the combustibility
Of anger and hatred.

People dislike others
Without even getting to know them,
Without even listening to them,
Without even giving them a chance.
Simply due to the fact
They are different.

Isolation, unhappiness, and loneliness
All become direct outcomes,
The absolute consequences,
The complete repercussions
Of these prejudices and emotions.

Yet simple acts of cooperation
Would help to overcome
So much of the distrust,
The suspicion and skepticism
That has evolved over the years.

Reaching out to one another
With small gestures,
With committed deeds,
With dedicated acts
Of kindness and compassion
Would quickly break down
The barriers we have built
Around ourselves and others.

How we prefer,
How we would like
To live the rest of our lives
Is up to completely up to us.

Always remember,
Each of us can make
Such a difference in the lives
Of those around us.

The choice is such
A simple one to make.
Do we choose confrontation
Or do we embrace cooperation?

The Puzzle

Our lives are like a puzzle
Each piece intricately
Fits into one another.
It takes years to put together.
It takes a lifetime to solve.

Each piece represents
A moment in our lives.
Each piece is a part of the whole.
If even a single segment is missing
The puzzle is incomplete.

Each segment of our journey.
From childhood
To the teenage years,
Through adulthood
Into the sunset span,
All come together to form
The perfect picture of our lives.

Happiness and sadness,
Love and hate,
Success and failure,
Peaceful solitude and lonely isolation,
Nature and nurture,
Are all individual fragments
Intricately woven together
Into the fabric of our lives.

It takes time to assemble
And organize the puzzle.
Putting each part into place
As the picture slowly
Emerges and shows itself
To the world.

When, at last, it is finished
And the puzzle is done.
We will leave behind
The complete picture,
The legacy of our lives
For others to see
And remember us by.

For it will be
The portrait of ourselves,
The story of our journey,
The one we created,
The one we put together
Throughout our lives.

Black Friday

In the darkness before dawn,
The lights of the mall shine brightly.
In one short day, our world has gone
From grateful to greedy.
As Thanksgiving has ended
And Black Friday has begun.

All the parking lots are full
With crazed drivers
Desperately trying to find a spot.
Outside the shops
Impatient people anxiously waiting
For the doors to open.
Once inside,
The insanity has built to a fever pitch
As shoppers outdo one another
Trying to uncover the best deals.

The pushing, the shoving, the
    rudeness
Merely to save a few dollars.
I watch in complete amazement
As absolute madness
Of Christmas shopping has begun.

The calm, loving family gatherings of
    yesterday
Have been replaced by the calamity of
    hysteria.
It is a completely different world
That has taken hold of the people
In the wild frenzy evolving around
    me.

Why am I here?
I really need nothing
But there is a morbid curiosity in
    witnessing
The swift, almost meteoric changing
    nature of humans
From one day to the next.
It is absolutely fascinating to watch
The dichotomy of two worlds
    colliding.

The masters of the mall
Have completed their task
In manipulating the population
And stirring them into the shopping
    frenzy
I am observing.

Before long,
It becomes too overwhelming
And I need to escape
To the quiet inner sanctum of my
    home and my bed
As the sun will not rise for hours.

Later, the scenes before me
Will be remembered and recalled
As a nightmarish dream.
One which I witnessed but quickly
    fled.
One which I will not revisit
Yet one which will occur again
Next year on Black Friday.

When Perception becomes Reality

Hidden deep within
Our utopian world
Of idealism and isolation
One can easily be fooled
By false promises,
Untruths and misconceptions.
Rumours and innuendos
Seems to have become the way
To communicate in today's world.

The truth, so difficult to uncover
Concealed and camouflaged
Hidden under layers of lies and deceit.
Very few take the time
To strip away the fiction
From the fact.

Everyday, there is an
Ever-increasing incongruence,
An ever-expanding chasm
Between the perception of fiction
And the reality of fact.

What we once perceived
To be our standard, unchangeable
  reality
Has been modified and mutated
Into an transformed and altered new
  normal.
One which contradicts and defies
All we have known and understood
Throughout our entire lives.
One which we may well
Be challenged by and struggle with
For the rest of our days.

We are now living in a world
Where our everyday life has become
  trapped
Within a new dimension, an unknown
  realm
Of continuous and ever-shifting
  reality.
One in which facts become
More difficult to believe
Than the fictions
That have been created.

We are being forced and must learn
To exist and survive in a world
Where fiction has become fact,
Where perception has become reality.
Where life as we have always
Known it to be
Has been changed forever.

Some Days

Some days
We are on top of the world
There is no challenge too great.
Everything we undertake
Will be accomplished with success.

Some days
The world weighs heavily
On our shoulders.
Apathy and inaction control our lives,
Motivation is impossible to find.

Some days
Life feels so good
Everything just seems to fall into
    place.
The sun is shining and we just know
The world is at it should be.

Some days
Life seems so bleak.
Each action takes such effort
The day is dark and gloomy.
The world is a complete mystery to
    us.
Some days
As we start our day
We have a feeling of serendipity
We know there is absolutely nothing
That will hold us back.

Some days
The isolation and loneliness
Supersedes and controls our lives
As a general malaise
Totally weighs us down.

Some days
The ride we take is so smooth,
Perfectly under control
One to be enjoyed
To the fullest.

Some days
The roller coaster
Is quickly moving totally out of
    control.
Never knowing what the next moment
May have in store for us.

As we travel though life,
We need to smooth out
The ride we are taking.
From day to day.
We have the ability to make
Bad days good
And good days even better.

Each and every day,
It is totally up to us
Our attitude towards life
Will determine how our days will be.
It is never easy
But we are definitely in control
For we truly are
The Masters of our own Destiny.

Time to Refocus

Our world seems to be
Upside down, inside out,
Confused beyond belief.
We have become lost
On the road of life,
We need a new map,
A new direction to follow.

Why are we so riveted on
The sensationalism of the slap?
On Chris and Will?
Instead of the kindness,
Respect and love
Between the Lady and Lisa?

Why do we spend so much time
Focussed on the negative
When there is so much
Positive to witness
In the world around us?

Our vision has become blurred.
We follow war instead of peace.
We watch hatred instead of love.
We observe ugliness instead of
    beauty.
We perceive complication instead of
    simplicity.
Quite simply,
We see black instead of white.

The time has come
To readjust our vision.
To refocus our lens,
To revise our view,
To sharpen our awareness.
To look for and to see
The good instead of the bad.

It is time for us
To ignore the slaps we witness,
To focus on the kindness, love and
    respect
That exists all around us.
It is time to walk down a new path,
To make the world a better place
For our children and grandchildren,
For all the generations
Who will follow us.

Why?

Dedicated to the children and their teachers
Who die so needlessly in gun violence.

Why does this continue to happen?
Time and again,
We witness, watch and cry over
The loss of pure innocence,
The destruction of incredible
    potential.
The death of unfulfilled promise.

In only an instant of time,
Again and again and again,
Lives are shattered, now and always.
Decency dies
Morality is murdered,
Integrity is destroyed
Never to be recovered.

Families are devastated, forever
    changed
A town mourns, mired in tragedy,
A state is distressed,
A country is grieving,
All of society is saddened,
Watching in silent shock,
Drowning in tears.

Yet, those who have
The power to act refuse to act.
Giving us excuses,
Simply justifying their existence,
Never facing the simple and basic
    truth.
Our children must be protected,
Our schools need to be safe,

For all of us,
The shock is overwhelming,
The silence is deafening,
The system is just not working.
Where is common sense?
It is time for action not rhetoric!

So many children taken from us,
So many families torn apart,
So many people unable to ever
    recover.
Over the years, they move forward,
But they are simply mere shadows
Reflecting lives that might have been.
Too many questions left without
    answers.

Life will go on
But it will never be the same,
Never escaping the stain inflicted.
Less innocence, more spiteful,
Less trusting, more suspicious,
Less confident, more insecurity.

Still, the question remains
Forever haunting our minds,
Forever touching our lives,
Forever stirring deep within our souls.
We did not know them
But we all cry tears of love
For each of them.
Forever left wondering,
Why does this continue to happen?

Biding Our Time

Another grey, dark and dingy day
With rain falling and wind blowing
    incessantly,
Mr puppies sleeping peacefully beside
    me.
There will be no walking today.

As the rain continues to fall
And the wind to blow,
It is all we have known
For days and weeks on end.

So many homes being flooded
As there is nowhere
For the water to go.
All of our lives being totally
    disrupted.

People have become
So unhappy, so negative, so
    pessimistic
Reflecting the gloom
Outside our windows.

With no end in sight.
Isolation and loneliness
Have become a way of life
For the past two years.

At first, a frightening pandemic
Running rampantly out of control.
Now, it is weather forcing us
To remain as isolated as before.

When will it end?
How much more can we take?
How does one fight against
The virus and the weather?

Both are formidable foes
On their own
But together, impossible to battle.
So, we are forced to wait,

Once again,
Our lives being put on hold,
Pausing until both storms
Finally come to an end.

Which we all know,
Eventually in time, they will.
Then, we will be able
To move forward with our lives.

However, all is not lost,
The grass has gone from brown to
    green.
The trees, once completely barren,
    now filled with leaves.
The last remnants of winter have been
    washed away.

So, for now,
All we can do
Is to wait,
Biding our time.

Another

Another journey completed,
Another dream fulfilled,
Another adventure comes to an end,
Another chapter closes in the story of
    our lives.

The journey has been long
With many twists and turns.
With many obstacles to overcome
But we have made it to the end.

The dream began so long ago.
We believed in what we could
    achieve.
It took focus, patience and love
But together we completed the dream.

We knew it would be an adventure
The unknown and unexplored path lay
    before us
But with commitment and desire, we
    followed it.
Others joined us and today the
    adventure ends.

The journey, the dream and the
    adventure
Have all become woven into the
    fabric of our lives.
The memories we have created will
    live on forever
As this chapter ends quietly and
    serenely today.

We will continue on.
Another journey, another dream,
Another adventure, another chapter
Will unfold as we move into the
    future together.

The Bullies

What is happening to our world?
The bullies are shouting louder than
    ever
Instead of being admonished,
They are applauded.
Instead of being avoided,
They are admired.

Their pulpits have become
The centre of attention.
Their lies have become
The new truth.
Their false words have become
The new reality.

The louder they shout,
The more they are heard.
They tear down so many others
To build themselves up.
Instead of being cast aside
They are exalted by the masses.

They get away with actions
For which the rest of us
Would be reprimanded.
They tear down the sacred institutions
Upon which our Nations have been
    built.
They live by their own rules.
They create their own realities.

They are blindly followed
By so many who do not understand
The dangerous precedent
They are setting.
Without fully comprehending
History can so easily
Repeat itself in the future.

The doctrines they espouse,
The damage they inflict
Will be felt for generations
Yet to come.
Affecting our children and
    grandchildren
For the rest of their lives.

There have always been bullies
But there have also been those
Who have stood up to them,
Not allowing dangerous changes
To be set in motion.

There have always been
Brave souls who fought against
The bullies of the past
Not allowing them to tread
On our rights and our freedoms.
Where are they?
For now is the time
We need them
More than ever
To come forward,
To speak out,
To stand up,
To repel the bullies.
Not allowing history
To repeat itself once again.

Section 12
Personal

Almost Seventy

When I look in the mirror
I see the eyes of a young man.
With deep lines of experience
Etched around them.
The shock of grey hair
Belying my belief of a lingering
    youth.
From time to time,
My body betrays me
With aches and pains
Not felt just a few years ago.

My memory,
Not quite as sharp as it once was.
Forgetting many simple things in
    daily life
Yet able to clearly recall
People, places and events
From fifty years ago.
Unable to fully fathom
That I have existed
For almost seventy trips
Around the sun.

No longer able to move as quickly
Nor enjoy the long-lasting energy
As I once had.
A constant fatigue had become
An ongoing fact of life.
My stamina eroded
By the years of maturity.
My body often unable
To do what my mind
Asks of it.

My senses, somewhat dulled,
By the ravages of the decades.
My vision blurred,
Not quite as clear.
My sense of smell
Not quite as acute.
My hearing
Diminished over time.
My actions and reactions
Slowed by the advance of age.

Yet,
I have so much to do
So many more experiences to enjoy,
With the time I have left.
So, with strong determination,
I will push through all
The shortcomings,
The imperfections,
The limitations
Of being almost seventy.

Fighting the Dragon

Dedicated to all Cancer Warriors

We must slay the dragon.
His relentless, unabated and
    unforgiving
Ferocity continues to grow
As time passes.
He hides away in his cave
Emerging whenever he pleases.

We are defenceless to his power.
Yet we must take on the quest
To confront and defeat
This dangerous menace.
He strikes without warning
No one is safe from his relentless
    attacks.

At his tenacious and insistent bequest
Those he calls must become warriors
Fighting an ongoing battle.
Giving up and giving in are just not
    options.
Although we do not see,
Do not understand,
Do not desire this confrontation
We have no choice but to take up
    arms.

To engage, to resist,
To defend ourselves,
To stand up to this bully.
We can not ignore him
Simply hoping,
He will give up and go away
He is deceptive,
He is devious,
He is deceitful
His pursuit is persistent,
It is never-ending.

We must be prepared to do
Whatever needs to be done,
Each and every day.
As we take on
This difficult and demanding
    challenge.
We need to know
We are not alone.
There are so many who will help us,
Standing beside us
As we wage this unwanted war,
Taking up arms against the dragon.

Allowing us
To move forward
To live our lives to the fullest
Giving us hope
When hope is most needed.
Giving us the desire
To battle on against all odds
Giving us stamina and the strength
To fight and defeat the dragon.

Lost in Life

Late at night,
Lying in the darkness
I often think
About close friends
Lost in time,
Lost in distance,
Lost in life.
Wondering if they
Ever think about me
As I think about them,
Recalling our time together.

In years long gone by,
Sharing our lives.
Then, slowly drifting apart
Into our own separate existence.
Never to be seen,
Never to laugh or cry together,
Never to be heard from
Never to share again
The close bond
That once tied us together.

We have moved on
But as I grow older,
I often reflect on
Where they may be,
How they lived their lives,
With whom they shared
The rest of their time.

Did they make the most
Of the friendships they made?
Or like us,
Did they simply
Drift away and disappear
Into the great abyss of their life?

Over the years
I have made many friends
Who have remained close
Who have stayed by my side
Sharing the moments of our lives,
Successes and failures,
Happiness and sadness
Good and bad times.

We have always been there
For each other
To love, to support, to share
Our ever-changing,
Always-challenging lives together.

Yet there are times
In the quiet darkness of the night
My mind recalls the life
Many years ago
Once shared with other close
    friendships
Now and forever,
Lost in time,
Lost in distance,
Lost in life.

A True Friend

To be a true friend,
You must to be able to speak exactly
The same words to someone's face
As you do behind their backs.
Too many people are faux friends
Saying but not believing their words.
Not believing in their hearts
The feelings they are expressing.
Often saying something that sounds
   good
But is not completely honest.

It is so much better
To have and to hold close
One or two true friends
Than possessing one hundred others.
A true friend is someone
Who will stand by your side
No matter the circumstances.
Someone who will stay with you
When others turn their backs,
When the tide of life flows against
   you.

Someone who will fight your battles
As if they were their own.
Someone who loves you
In spite of your follies and
   weaknesses.
Someone who quite simply
Likes you for who you are
Not for who others want you to be.
Someone who loves and believes in
   you
Even when you do not love
Or believe in yourself.

True friends are like rare gems.
Very difficult to find,
Often missed in the maze of life.
Yet when discovered and uncovered
Remain precious and will be treasured
Throughout your life.
Growing closer and more valuable,
Over time and the passing of years.
Making your life so much more
   special
Than it would ever be without them.

The Battle

When you fight the battle,
You have to do
All that needs to be done.
Whatever it takes
Each and every day,
Never letting up.

Be it your mind or your health,
Always moving forward,
Staying positive,
Never allowing yourself
To fall into the black hole
Of self doubt, pity or recrimination.

Living your life,
As best you can.
Controlling your disease
Never letting your disease
Control your life.
Enjoying the little things,
Always staying within yourself,
Taking it one step at a time.

As a warrior,
Never giving up the fight!
For it is a formidable foe
You are facing
But one that must be controlled.
Allowing you to do
What you want to do
When you want to do it.

Living your life one day at a time.
Not letting your imagination
Create perceptions
That may never become realities.
Not allowing your mind
To create an imaginary, fictitious
    future.

Living in the moment,
For we never know
What lies ahead.
Sometimes it is difficult
To accept the hand
You have been dealt.
For it may not be
What you expected
Or what you had hoped for.
But always remembering,
It is what it is!

Striving to control the controllable,
Letting the rest go.
Focussing on what is important
For you to live your life
To the very fullest,
To be at your best.

Fighting the battle
With all you have.
Knowing you have support
Of others around you.
Understanding that life is good,
Feeling things will get better,
Sensing you have so much
To look forward to
As you move towards your future.

Twilight Time

Twilight time,
That special time of day
When the sun
Rests gently on the western horizon,
Bathing the world below
In it's golden glow.

When a quiet solitude
Descends and surrounds us
With a feeling of peaceful tranquility
As another day comes to an end.

For many of us,
The twilight time of our lives,
A time to rest
At the end of our long journey.

A time to bask
In the glow of the times
We have shared
With so many others.

A time to remember
The days gone by.
A time to reflect
On the story we have written.

Finally allowing ourselves
To relax and enjoy the evening,
The autumn of our lives.
Before we reach the end
Of the path we have travelled.

Looking back
On the narrative already completed
Looking forward
To creating new chapters
Before our book is finished.

Twilight time,
That golden time of day,
That golden time of our lives
A time of friendship and family,
A time of excitement and enjoyment,
A time of adventure and anticipation.

The Disease

It is a battle
Each and every day.
During the day
I am distracted
By the activities of life
But at night
In the dark and lonely solitude
When sleep does not come easily
Or if it does,
It is only short lived.

In the deep silence
When symptoms
Decide to act up,
When my mind starts
To play games
When mind and body
Refuse to work together.
When I am at fragile moments.

It is then
When my doubts crescendo,
When I am at my weakest
When night sweats are at their worst
When I know I must fight on
And not give in to the disease.
It is then
When I see me as alive
But the disease
Sees other options,
None of which
Are palatable to me.

People always mean well
Asking how I am,
Telling me I look so well.
I bite my tongue
Knowing the absolute truth
Would not sit well
With the questioner.

Knowing, day by day
The disease is more than likely
Winning the battle
In spite of my efforts
To delay the inevitable outcome.

With this disease
Perception on the outside
Often is not the same
As the reality within.
I continue
To live my life
To the fullest
Knowing that the finish line
May well be much closer
Then I would like to believe.

When we were young
We always thought
We would live forever.
But now
With the disease raging
I realize life is precious,
Much shorter then forever.

Sometimes sensing
The finish line
Is within sight.
Always hoping to push
The inevitable
Far off into the future.
While knowing deep within
That will just not happen.

All I can do is
Know, accept and understand
It is what it is
One step at a time,
One day at a time.

Section 13
Night Time

The Nocturnal Battle

It is four o'clock in the morning.
I should be sleeping.
But my mind is racing,
Overflowing with useless information
That should not be
Even be acknowledged,
Much less gathering and expanding,
Interrupting my sleep.

It is like this
Almost every night.
At any moment when I awaken
Something triggers
An endless flow of information,
A torrential river of thoughts,

Most of them,
Confusing and mundane,
Jumbled together
In a complicated jigsaw puzzle
That must be solved immediately.

Now is not the time
To settle the battles of my life
Nor the woes of the world.
Yet my mind is trying
To do just that.
Now should be the time
For restful repose
Preparing for the day ahead.

Thus, the battle rages between
My mind and my body.
The rest my body needs
Appears to be
Unimportant and unnecessary
To my active mind.

It seems the more
I try to relax
New confusing patterns of thoughts
Are released by my subconscious,
Flooding, disturbing and disrupting
My conscience mind.

As I slowly try
To sort through
The sea of redundant information
I sense my tired body
Fighting back,
Starting to relax.

Before long,
The information flow
Within my mind
Is becoming less clear,
More confusing
Until the tipping point is reached

As it all turns off,
I fall into a slumber.
Hoping it will last
Until morning.
But knowing full well,
It may not.
And so, the battle will continue…

The End of the Night

The sky above me is an inky black
With just a faint hint of light
As a sliver of grey
Appears at the edge
Of the eastern horizon.
The planets and stars
Still twinkling translucently
High above where I walk.

Nothing is stirring yet
As the dark veil of stillness
Envelopes me.
The world is still at rest,
At peace for this brief moment.

The trees look foreboding
As silhouettes of darkness
Give them an eerie presence
As I wander by.
The mockingbirds, still sleeping,
Have yet to begin their morning
    songs.
No animals are moving,
Even the wind is still.

Walking at this early hour
Gives me a feeling of euphoric joy,
A sense of serene serendipity,
An enjoyment of soundless solitude,
Felt at no other time of day.
I am alone in the world
For this brief period of time.

I move slowly
Relishing the sound of silence
Which surrounds me.
Realizing, before long,
The world will awaken
For another day.

But in this muted moment,
It is just me,
Walking slowly,
Appreciating the peaceful isolation
Of another night
Coming to an end.

Night Battle

Inky blackness surrounds me
As I lie in a cold sweat,
My body and bed sheets,
Completely soaked,
While I tremble and shake
With distress and discomfort.

The only sound is
The constant whirring of a fan
As it blows back and forth,
Cooling me down.
While deep in the darkness
This dreaded disease takes control
Of my body.
The aches and pain,
Hidden away by the light of day,
Emerge in the night.

While my restless mind,
Works overtime,
Making sleep impossible,
As scenes which may never occur
Unfold before me
Not allowing me to find
The rest I need and crave.

During this quiet time of night,
The tense battle rages between us
On the brink of uncertainty and self-
    doubt.
Fantasy, the prince of darkness,
Takes over,
Pushing aside the realism
That will reign in the light of day.

For this is the only time
When I allow
The anxiety and apprehension
Of my future to emerge.
When the disease
Confronts and challenges me.
In the weakness of this moment
My strength to battle wanes
As my confused and vivid
    imagination
Runs rampant.

Until at last
Fatigue and drowsiness
Wear me down
And I fall into another short, fitful
    sleep
Knowing tomorrow, once again,
I will control my disease,
Living my life to the fullest.

Dark Shadows

Lying awake,
In a unsettled state
As dark shadows
Surround me.
Invading my mind
In the middle of the night.

Clouding my vision,
Creating confusion,
Crowding my judgement.

Dark shadows guiding me
Down a path
I do not want to travel.

Innocent pictures of my life
Replaced by menacing mental
    creations.
Clear thinking
Replaced by fear of the unknown.
Happiness and joy
Replaced by a deep foreboding
    melancholy.

Dark shadows
Building a wall of deep regret
Reminding me of images
I wish to forget.
Fear holding me in place
Afraid to move forward.

For now, I am forced
To remain in this state
Of mental frigidity.
Frozen in place,
Silently waiting for daylight
To warm me, releasing me
From these dark shadows,
From these feelings of anxiety.
Clearing the path,
Allowing me to move forward
To face another day.

1159PM

As I stare at my bedside clock,
It is 1159 PM.
In just one short minute
Tomorrow will become today,
Today will turn into yesterday,
Yesterday will be two days ago.

And, once a year,
When tomorrow becomes today,
It is a year later.
When next year is suddenly this year.
As this year turns into last year,
And last year fades into our past.

Days quickly pass by
Turning into weeks,
Weeks into months
And months into years.
As we get older,
Time seems to move
So much more rapidly
Than when we were young.

Never stopping to rest
For even one minute.
The future becomes the present,
The present turns into the past
And the past quietly converts
Into a distant memory.

The merry-go-round of time
Never slowing down,
Always continuing
As life moves forward.
One day fades into the next,
One week, one month, one year.
Year after year, time goes on.

We have no choice, no control
As we are forced to move with it.
Often never even noticing
We are slowing down
In mind and in body.
Time does not change
But we do.

As we advance into
Another phase of our life
From childhood to youth,
Quickly becoming an adult
Then suddenly, a senior
In the sunset stage of our lives.

One day, without warning,
The merry-go-round will suddenly
    stop.
Time will no longer move forward.
We will have reached
The end of the path,
The end of our long journey.

So, may the memories
We create day after day be those
We will want to recall tomorrow
When tomorrow becomes today,
Today becomes yesterday,
And yesterday disappears into our
    past.

May we want to always remember
And be remembered by others
For the merry-go-round events
We created during our ride though
    life.

The Single Beam

The pale light from the full moon
Casts an illumination across my bed
Giving me a sense of security and
    stability
In a world of disorder and disarray.

The single beam is the only
    luminescence
In my domain of darkness.
The only clarity showing me the way
Through the uncertainty and
    confusion.

A shining candle, guiding me,
Helping me, giving me hope
To overcome all the obstacles
Lying ahead in the path of my life.

Quietly realizing in the desolate
    silence
That I can and will find my way
Through the dark shadows of the
    present
Into the bright certainty of the future.

Section 14
Family

Forever Changed

Dedicated to all new mothers

Your life has been
Forever changed
So many things
You have always done
You will never do again
But in their place
So many new exciting
Things to do.

You will never be alone
As you start your new life.
For there is now someone
Who depends totally on you.
Someone you will love
With all your heart,
With all you are,
With all you will become.

A responsibility
So much more important
Than any other
You have ever had.
Raising another
To be a good, happy and decent
    person
Will take care and love,
Patience and understanding
But you will give all these
Without any hesitation
For the rest of your life.

Over the many years ahead,
At times, your relationship
Will be challenged,
Will evolve,
Will change
But this little one
Will always be
The most important person
In your life
And you in theirs.

Yes, your life has been
Forever changed
So many things
You have always done
You will never do again
But in their place
So many new exciting
Things to do.
For now, you are a mother.

A Parents Prayer

When you are hungry
I will feed you.
When you cry
I will comfort you
When you laugh
I will share the joy with you.
When you sleep
I will watch over you.

When you are in pain
I will give you solace.
When you are filled with fear
I will safeguard you.
When you want to learn
I will teach you.
When you search for answers
I will help you.
When you feel danger,
Real or perceived,
I will protect you.

As you explore the world around you
I will share your curiosity.
I will see
The beauty of the clouds
Through your eyes.
I will feel
The softness of a kitten's fur
Though your fingers.
I will hear
The robin's joyful song
Through your ears.
I will smell
The fragrance of the lilac
Through your nose.
I will taste
The sweetness of honey,
The bitterness of salt
Through your tongue.

Without hesitation,
Without question
Without doubt
I will share my life with you.
I will give you
Whatever you need
For as long as you need it.
I will always be there for you,
Standing by your side,
As you face
The peaks and valleys of your life.

When the time comes,
Without prejudice, without coercion,
With love, with trust, with faith,
I will give you
The freedom to make
The choices you desire.
I will advise and assist
Only when you ask.
I will support and defend you,
I will walk beside you
On the path through life
You choose to follow.
I wish for you
Happiness, peace and contentment
Throughout the course of your life.

Just One Short Day

Wide awake so very early in the
    morning,
Excited about the prospect of
    spending
This special day with my family.
As the world around us, once again,
Closes down with the distress and
    panic
Of yet another wave of the pandemic.

This never-ending, always-present,
Completely encompassing,
    challenging chaos
That continues to threaten, disrupt
And change our normal everyday
    lives.
Yet today will be one day
When we will be able to overcome
And set aside all the negativity
    surrounding us.

Today will be a day of giving and
    forgiving,
A day to enjoy the solitude of sharing.
For all children and for the rest of us
It is a special day.
For many, it has deep religious
    meaning
For others, just a special day
Of peace and tranquility.

When we will put aside
The troubles of our lives
To enjoy the company of those we
    love,
Holding them close.
Sharing a few quiet hours together.
For tomorrow, once again,
We will face the demands and
    challenges
Of the world around us

But today we can isolate ourselves
On an island of love and hope.
Leaving far behind us
The trepidation, fear and anxiety
We confront all other days of the year.

For today is Christmas Day,
Like so many others around the
    world,
I am ready to take the time
To simply enjoy the happiness
Life has given me with those I love
    most,
Hidden away for just one short day.

The Common Bond

It was a day of sharing,
A day of caring.
It was a gathering of family,
A gathering filled with love,
Filled with hope.
It was a time of giving,
A time for forgiving

Once a year for a single day
Just a few hours spent together.
Coming together from many miles apart.
Pushing aside the distance between us,
Putting aside the differences in our lives.

Accepting each other
For who we are,
For who we want to be,
Sharing the tales of our lives,
Both past and present.
Telling the stories of our hopes,
Our dreams for the future.

Allowing us to be ourselves
Without any prejudices,
Without any preconceptions
Of who we have been,
Who we should be
Who we may become.

All coming together
With our own experiences in life,
Our own belief systems,
So different, so diversified
Always being challenged and changed
By the influences of nature and nurture.

Yet sharing a common bond
One that can never be broken
Tied together forever by blood.
Allowing our similarities to shine through,

Our differences hidden away for just
    one day.
Then, quietly and quickly returning,
Once again, to our own lives,
Our own experiences,
Our own existences.

Knowing there will always be
Another time,
Another day to come back together.
Wanting it to happen,
Waiting for it to occur,
Willing it to take place,
A time for our family to gather,
To love, to hope,
To appreciate one another.

By then, another year will have
    passed,
We will have been changed
By the differences, the contrasts in
    our lives
Yet the camaraderie will hold strong
When, once again, the family will
    gather together,
Sharing our love, our lives,
Our hopes and our dreams for the
    future.

People, so divergent, so varied
Yet so similar, so close,
So alike, always knowing
Year after year, throughout our lives.
The common bond of family
Bringing us together,
Holding us strong
Not unlike and no different from
So many other families around the
    world.

A Father's Poem

I am sorry and always will be
We never really fully reconciled.
For, at that time,
There was just so much history
Established over so many years.
Having built a wall
Too high to overcome,
Having created a barrier
Too impenetrable to break through,
Having erected a roadblock
Too wide to circumvent.

In many ways,
I must and will take
My share of the blame
For being
Too young, too stubborn, too
    immature
To attempt to settle our differences.

Just as you were too old,
Too set in your ways
To lean towards reconciliation.
Yet, at the same time,
I am forever grateful
You were able to have
Better and stronger relationships
With my younger siblings.

I am grateful they were with you
Sharing stories,
Sharing music,
Sharing love
As you passed from this life.

Despite our differences,
As I grow older
And move into my sunset years,

I look in the mirror of my life
Recognizing and realizing
How much I am like you
In so many ways.

Your strengths and your weaknesses
Live on in me,
Live on in all your children.
You may be gone
But your influence is hidden
Deep within each of us.
For that is the way it should be,
A parent living on in their children.

You will always be remembered
Differently by each of us.
Our memories may be unique
But you will be celebrated
As we relive and tell
Our own stories about you.
Passing them on to our children,
As they will in time,
Pass on stories about us to theirs.
Perhaps, that is the most important
    thing
As we move from generation to
    generation.

So, in the end,
I will and must
Thank you for being you.
For you have influenced who I am,
The person I have become.
Just as my children
Will carry me with them
For the rest of their lives
When I am gone.

My True Family

As I grow older
I have come to accept the fact
That blood does not make a family.
Blood gives a false expectation of
    closeness.
So often in life
Creating an undue pressure to those
    relationships
Which over time,
Will shatter beyond repair and
    reconciliation.

I have come to realize
More often than not
Family are those you choose
And who choose you
To be a part of their lives.
Developing a bond of friendship and
    love
Over the years far stronger
Than any ties of blood.

My true family are those
Who have given my unconditional
    support
Without expectation over the years.
Accepting me for who I am
With all my weaknesses and my
    fragilities.
Allowing me to be the person I must
    be.
Not trying to create a false idol,
A mere image, an unsubstantiated
    impression.

Blood is not a choice
But true friendship and love is.
Therein, lies the difference!
Therein, lies the truth!
Therein, lies the freedom!

For it is friendship and love
Not blood that creates a true family.
One that will endure
Over the many years.
One that will last
Through the good times and bad,
Looking forward to the future,
Working together to make our lives
    better.

Being a Grandparent

A wrinkled hand,
To tenderly guide you.
A withered smile
To warm your heart.
A tender word
To heal your wounds.
A twinkle in their eyes
To lovingly tease you.
An active and vibrant mind
To share a lifetime of experience.

A body, worn by the decades
Yet always ready to assist.
Walking slower, less steadily
Yet always there to lean on.
Someone filled with empathy,
To share your happiness
And dry your tears.

Older, wiser, more patient,
Ready to teach new generations,
To lead them along the path of life.
To help them avoid the pitfalls,
To overcome the barriers,
To dream and to fulfill those dreams.

Before their journey ends,
Ensuring those they love
Will be ready take up the torch
And move forward with their lives.
Teaching them
To be good to others,
To share their experience
With the future generations,
To love and to be loved.

Gently and quietly,
Leading by example
As they were led
So many years ago
By their grandparents.
Passing on their knowledge,
Their experience,
Their passion,
Their love of life.

Who Was The One?

Who was the one who
Gave you butterfly kisses
Before you went to sleep?
Would read the same story
Night after night?
Would check under your bed
To scare away any monsters?
Held you tight and protected you
From the world with his big bear
    hugs?

Who was the one who
Was there to dry your tears
When you fell?
Told you terrible punny Dad jokes
Just you make you smile?
Stared into the night sky
Teaching you about the stars,
The planets and the worlds beyond

Who was the one who
Who wore a tiara for tea parties?
Took you on special Daddy Daughter
    Dates?
Slow danced as you stood on his feet?
Watched your favourite cartoon or
    movie
Over and over and over again?

Who was the one who
Would dress up as Santa each year
To make Christmas extra special?
Breathlessly ran beside you
On your first bike ride
Without training wheels?

Who was the one who
Loved you the first time
He laid eyes on you?
Who cried silently behind a closed
    door
When as a teenage
You told him you hated him?
Will always unconditionally love
And be there for you?

Who was the one who
Proudly watched you sing and dance
Always celebrating your successes,
Commiserating your failures.
Was always there to hear about
Your new found loves and
    heartbreaks?
Then, when the time came
Walked you down the aisle
To give you away to another?

Who was the one who
Over many years
Did all this without hesitation,
With happiness, compassion and love
Because that's what a father does
And will always do for his little one!

Section 15
Childhood

The Toddler

Dedicated with love and hugs
To my Grandson Levi on his 1st
Birthday

As a one year old, so intensely
  curious,
Continuously exploring the world
  around him.
Quickly crawling from one place to
  another,
Pulling everything within his reach
  onto the floor.
So many things we take for granted
He sees through young eyes
Filled with a zealous, impassioned
  interest.
Everything is so exciting to him,
Just waiting to be discovered,
  investigated and inspected.

Quietly reading with his mother or
  father,
Eyes filled with anticipation and
  amusement,
Looking at the pictures in front of
  him.
Preparing for another nap time.
Then, crying and calling out,
The moment he wakes up.
Always ready to, once again,
Begin searching for and
Uncovering new adventures.

His canine brother always loves meal
  time
Eagerly and instantly cleaning up
  around him.
As so much more ends up on the floor
Than ever gets into his mouth.
His best friend, Charlie, a large dog,

So protective, so gentle.
Allows him to do just about anything
So patient, so understanding.

Such a simple, uncomplicated life,
Everything is so new to him.
Loving, laughing, learning
A little sponge absorbing all.
He communicates with everyone
In his own intimate, natural way.
Quickly becoming frustrated
When those around him
Do not immediately understand
What he is trying to say.

For a few moments,
Sitting quietly playing in his playpen
Until he pulls himself up.
Circling round and round,
Continually throwing his toys in all
  directions.
His smile constantly lighting up the
  room
Making everyone happy.
His laugh and his giggles
Bringing joy to all around him.

During quiet time
At the end of each day
Sitting contentedly in a lap,
Listening and learning,
For soon, he will fall asleep
Dreaming about new adventures
  tomorrow.
He is growing so quickly,
Changing so much,
Understanding more each day.
Before long, he will be ready to move
Into the next stage of his life.

Through the Eyes of a Child

The experiences of our lives
Often leave us
Cynical and sceptical.
So we tend to view
The world around us
Though jaded eyes.
We miss the simple pleasures
As we look with indifferent, clouded
    lenses.

Take the time to watch a child
As they explore the world
Without expectation,
Without prejudice,
Without judgement.
They can vividly see and enjoy
All those simple things
We often overlook as adults

As they walk along
A path through the woods,
They watch in wonder
As butterfly passes by.
They laugh gleefully
As they see a family of ducks
Simply floating on the water.
They clap their hands with delight
At flowers blooming around them,
At the birds flying overhead,
At the squirrels scampering by.

All of these natural events
Intensifies an incredible sense
Of happiness and excitement
Within a child.
The world is theirs to explore
As they wander through it.
Each new experience
Brings them absolute uninhibited joy.

With curiosity leading the way,
Pulling them forward
To look even more closely
At this wonderful world,
New and unknown to them.
Everything is waiting
To be fully investigated
As the wonders of nature
Unfold before them.

The animals and birds,
The flowers and fauna,
The sky above and
The terrain beneath their feet,
So often ignored by us,
Simply passed by as adults
Are all closely observed by a child.

Perhaps, it is time for us
To look at the world
Through new lenses.
To put aside
All the doubts and distrusts of
    adulthood,
To see everything
Through the eyes of a child.

The Gang of Five

Back in the early 60s
In a small Ontario town
There were five of us.
We ruled the boulevard
Or so we thought.
For when you are six years old,
There is nothing holding you back.

It was an age of innocence
When one could wander
The streets at any time
Of day or night
Without fear
And we were fearless.
Daring each other
To do the impossible,
Always allowing our imaginations
To soar with new adventures.

We were young
Without the worries of the world
Weighing heavily on our shoulders.
Looking back, history tells us
There were things happening
In the world around us
But we didn't know
Or care about them.

We lived our lives,
Fought our imaginary battles
Against unseen foes.
Always uncovering new adventures,
Always supporting,
Having each other's backs
Through thick and thin.

Now, in the sunset years of my life
I look back to those times
We shared together.
Remembering, reflecting

On all the fond memories
We created in our childhood.
Those were good years,
Years of friendship,
Of fellowship,
Of camaraderie,
Of togetherness.

Then, the reality of our lives took
    over
And we went our separate ways.
As so often is the case
We grew apart,
We lost touch,
The closeness and innocence
We shared at six years old
Was gone, simply disappeared.

Like so many others,
We made new friends,
Formed new relationships
Moved on with our lives
But the memories
Of those first childhood friendships
Always remained,
Lying dormant in our minds,
Waiting be rekindled
One day in the future.

For those early life bonds
Are never forgotten.
They are always remembered
Like a pleasant dream
One has from time to time.
Awakening from a nightly slumber
With such good feelings,
With a sense of serendipity.
For we were
And always will be
The Gang of Five.

Becoming a Toddler

He is such an amazing little human
    being!
Changing from a totally dependent
    baby
Sleeping in his mother's arms
Just a few short months ago,
He is starting to find his way in the
    world

Surrounded by the love of his parents,
He is learning to experiment,
To try new things
Each and every day.
He is truly one of the wonders of life.

Before they know it,
He will be crawling and, then, walking.
Exploring the world around him
With an ever-growing fascination
And sense of awe and amazement.

There are so many changes
Taking place all at once
As he becomes a toddler and masters
Moving himself around his world,
Already belly-crawling, propelling
    himself
Towards one of his toys.

Learning to feed himself
With more landing on the floor
Than in his mouth
Which his big brother,
The dog, sees as a blessing
Always there to assist when needed.

To talk, to express himself
Using his own language
With the complete expectation
It is up to the rest of us
To fully understand
What he is trying to communicate.

Each day, each week, each month
He is changing and developing
With such incredible speed.
It is a challenge for those
Who love him most
To keep up with him.

Having been through this before,
I understand the process has barely
    begun
But the love he shares
With everyone around him
Turns this challenge into an
    opportunity
Which will become an easy burden to
    bear
Throughout the years ahead.

Our Children

Children should be
Living their lives
Not fighting for them.
They should be
Running, playing, laughing,
Even getting into trouble
Like all other children.

Yet so many are fighting,
Each and every day.
With smiles on their brave faces,
With determination in their eyes
With hope in their hearts
All the while, living with pain,
As they battle on.

We need to be there for them
Helping in every way we can.
Standing beside them,
Joining them in their fight.
They can not do it alone.
Together, we can make
Such a difference in their lives!

We can, we must and we will
Be there for them.
To walk beside them,
Holding their hands,
Helping them
Every step along the way.
Guiding them along
The path of their lives

To always ensure
Their love, their laughter
Their hopes and their dreams
Continue to thrive and to grow
For many years to come!

We must always remember
That our children
Should be living their lives,
Loving their lives
Not fighting for them!

Fight For The Children!

Now is the time to join together
And help the children fighting cancer.
They should be living their lives
Not fighting for them!

Each and every day,
These brave little souls
Are confronting battles
No child should have to endure.

Their families, always supporting
   them,
Sadly watching, waiting, wondering
As they endure pain and suffering
No child should have to live through.

Yet, with a smile on their faces
They fight on!
Never hesitating, never faltering,
Never giving up hope.

Only hidden deep in their eyes
Can one see the pain within
As they battle an unwavering,
Unforgiving, unrelenting foe.

They should not,
They must not
Be left alone, on their own,
To fight this endless battle.

It is up to each of us
To join them.
To help them in any way we can
To give them the opportunity they
   deserve.

All they want to do
Is to live a normal life
Like any other child
To laugh, to play and to love.

Together, we can make such a
   difference
In the lives of these young children.
Now is the time for all of us to join
   them
In the Fight Against Kid's Cancer!

Cry For The Children!

As a nation,
We have been tainted.
We have been stained.
We have been disgraced.
So many years ago
But for so many
Time stands still.
A Generation forever
Lost in time.

Under the guise of righteous religion
So many misguided men and women
Living inhumane and inhuman lives
Hidden away
From the rest of the world
Blindly trusted to do
What was the best
For the children.
All the while
Abusing those in their care.

So many children gone,
Lost forever.
Numbers which will never
Be fully known or understood.
Defenceless children,
Now and forever,
Lying in unmarked graves.

So many unfaithful,
Untrustworthy, irresponsible adults
Taking away
The innocence of childhood.
Taking away
All their future hopes and dreams.
Taking away
The potential of a generation.

Now, we are left to mourn
With so many unanswered questions.
We are left with anger and frustration,
With the senselessness of what
    happened.
We are left with the hopelessness
Of an undeniable and uncontrollable
    situation.

All we can do is
Cry for the children
Hoping to wash away
The irrefutable and inexcusable stain
From our history.
Knowing the memory
Of those countless children lost
Will remain with us forever.
So, we are left to
Cry for the children!

Section 16
Inspiration

Inspiration and Imagination

Inspiration and imagination
Limitless and without boundaries,
Are always alive within us
Just waiting to be released.
They cost nothing,
Everyone has complete access to
    them.

If we just open up our minds and our
    hearts
To the world around us,
Liberating inspiration and imagination
We can inspire, uplift and motivate
    each other
To be and to feel better
Even during our darkest hours.

Helping one another
Through the even most difficult of
    days.
Inspiration can be found
In the most simple of things in our
    lives
And when combined with one's
    imagination
A powerful stimulus is created.

When we can feel other people's
    words,
When we see the world through their
    eyes
When we walk the path beside them,
All of our lives become better.

Combining inspiration with
    imagination
Gives us the freedom,
The opportunity and the possibility,
To bring light into the darkness
Surrounding us.
To feel a sense of togetherness
While totally isolated and alone.
To move away from the inactivity of
    apathy
Taking action to help others around
    us.
To uplift our spirits
When we are at our lowest point.
To bring happiness and joy
During a time of sorrow and
    depression.
To give us strength
Whenever we feel weak.

Just a small spark of inspiration
Can light the fire of imagination,
Igniting the flames of hope and
    anticipation
Encouraging, motivating and inspiring
    us to dream
As we move together
Towards a greater and brighter future.

Writing the Book

Sunrise, as each day
The eastern horizon springs to life
Arising from the darkness of the
    night.
Awakening the world from it's deep
    slumber,
The dawn of a new day
Allowing us to move forward,
Leaving the past behind,
The chance to build a better future,
Giving us the opportunity
To change the chapters of our lives,
To create a new history for ourselves,
To construct a new path to follow.

Sunset, as each evening
The western horizon lights up
With an array of dramatic colours
Before darkness takes over
Plunging the world
Into the dark shadows of the night.
Allowing us to rest from the labours
    of the day
To regenerate, rekindling our passion
For the lives we are leading.
To remember the successes, to recall
    the failures,
A time to dream
Of the unlimited opportunities lying
    ahead.

Sunrise,
The regeneration of life each day
Offering us the excitement of the
    unknown.
Sunset,
The closing of a page
Preparing us to write a new one
    tomorrow.

Sunrise,
Giving us a sense of hope, to
    anticipate
That today will be better than
    yesterday,
Sunset,
Allowing us to visualize, to imagine,
    to dream,
That tomorrow will be better than
    today.

Each sunrise,
A new beginning to be written.
Each sunset,
The end of a single page.
Sunrise, sunset, sunrise, sunset,
The never-ending flow
As we develop and shape
The books of our lives.

We are the authors, the playwrights
    and the poets.
We are the ones who generate the
    words
To be written on each page, in each
    chapter
Within the books we are creating.
Every sunrise and sunset
Gives us a new beginning and an end.
But it is absolutely up to us
To fill in all the words,
To design and to complete the book.

A Single Spark

Just a single spark of discontent
Can ignite the flames of passion
To change the world and the course of
   history
As the storm clouds gather,
The mistakes of our past surround us.
Sudden flashes of the lightning
Of unrest, impatience and anger
Strike nervousness and fear into the
   hearts
Of even the bravest men.

The dynamic, shifting movement of
   our lives
Heading uncontrollably into a new
   direction
Brings on a sense of instability.
An uncertainty, an insecurity
Of what the future may hold for us.
That precarious feeling
We are standing, wavering, teetering
On the edge of a cliff of skepticism
With only the abyss of the unknown
   far below.

For now, there is no turning back,
As the strong winds
Of resentment and unhappiness,
Ever-increasing, swirl wildly around
   us.
We are swept up
In the tensions of the unresolved,
The unpredictability of a path,
Never before seen or followed,
Just waiting to be explored.

Hesitancy and indecision,
Doubt and vacillation,
Are no longer options.
The time has come for us to move
   forward.
To redraft the fallacies and faults of
   the past,
To rewrite the way we think and act,
To revise the route we will follow.
To rescript the course of history.

As the fires of change are raging,
The inferno of passion has been
   ignited,
The inflamed explosion of excitement
All created by a single spark.
Lighting the path ahead,
Directing, leading and pushing us
Towards a new and unfamiliar world.
This escalating futuristic fire all began
With just a single spark of discontent.

A Mirror

I often wonder why people
Read the words I write.
Why do they react as they do?
How am I able to touch their hearts
With my musings about life?

I simply write about
My experiences each day.
There is nothing complicated or
    contrived.
I write as I observe, as I feel,
As I encounter, as I confront

The happiness, the sadness,
The honesty, the hypocrisy,
The success, the failure,
The simple and the complex.

The loneliness, the companionship,
The depression, the cheerfulness,
The indifference, the emotion,
The apathy and the enthusiasm

All of which
Are a part of our lives.
For there is so much
To be seen, heard and felt
Around us each and every day.

Sometimes,
We are in control of our lives
At other times,
We are controlled by them.

Some thoughts, some things,
We accept without question
While others,
We reject and fight against
For all we are worth

But all of these,
We must try to understand.
We need to take the time
To watch the mystery
Of the world and our lives
As they unfold before us.

So, the question remains.
Why do people read the words I
    write?

Perhaps, it is because
I am simply a mirror,
Showing them the reflections
Of what they themselves
See, hear, feel and touch
In their own lives.

Supporting them with empathy,
Uplifting their spirits when they are
    down,
Giving them hope for their future,
Showing them the path forward
Motivating them to keep going.

Helping them to understand
No matter what happens in their lives
We are all going through it together.
Perhaps as they read my words
They realize, accept and appreciate
They are never alone.

You Can Cope with Hope

No matter what challenges
Life throws at you.
Whether they are
Large or small,
Mind or body,
Real or imagined.

When the mountain appears too high
The valley too deep,
The river too wide
When the challenges
Seem to be
Impossible, inconceivable,
    insurmountable,
When you feel they are
Unworkable, unimaginable,
    unachievable.

There is always hope.
For it is hope
Which will give you
The ability to cope.

For with hope,
Opportunities, options and choices
Will always emerge
To help you manage, control and
    conquer.

You will be able to climb
The highest of mountains.
Forge the deepest of valleys.
Swim the widest of rivers.

Hope will always give you
The power to cope,
The ability to overcome,
The strength to move forward.
All it takes is just a little hope
To break through
Whatever appears to be impossible.

No matter
How high, how deep or how wide
The challenge before you may look
With hope, you can overcome
Any hardship or handicap
Any barrier or blockade,
Any drawback or deterrent,
Any hurdle or hinderance.

With hope,
You have the ability
To see past the present
To move towards the future.
You will not only survive
But will thrive.
Growing stronger
From the obstacles and challenges
Blocking your path.
Hope will always give you
The strength and the ability to cope.

Always Alliteration

Always writing with alluring
    alliteration,
Using such a potentially powerful tool
Beautifully bringing the reader
Phrases to ponder,
Images to ignite imagination,
Eliciting an emotional empathy
Through the writer's words.

Dutifully describing while
Skillfully scribed to set the story,
Taking the reader on a joyous journey
Emoting an emotional energy
For the talented tale
Uniquely unfolding before them.

The reader is ready
To willingly wander
Into the writer's world
Through the pictures painted
On the printed pages before them.

As they read,
They walk with the witty wordsmith
And they dare to dream
About the wonderful world waiting
To be explored.

Always pondering which path,
Which passage to follow.
Being lovingly led
Along the way with words,

Energetically expressing and
    emphatically encouraging,
While regularly reminding the reader
    to remember
Life must be lived and loved
With empathy each and every day,
Moving forever forward into the
    future.

Let's Talk!

There are so many people struggling
During these difficult and challenging
    times.
So many, left alone,
Isolated, lonely and depressed.
We all need to take the time
To reach out, to talk,
To share and to care.

It takes so little
To do so very much.
Each one of us
Can make such a difference
In one another's lives
If we will just
Take the time to reach out.

All we need to do is to
To let others know
They are never alone.
We are here for them
Ready to talk,
Ready to help
In any way we can.

It has been said
By someone far wiser
Than this poet
That "No man is an island".
Words so true need
To be heard and acted upon
By each and every one of us.
We can not wait,
We can not procrastinate.
Now is the time to take action,
To help one another.

If you are someone
Who needs to talk,
Please reach out!
Make the move
For there is always someone
Who is here to help you.
All you have to do is ask.

So, let's all take the time
To talk to someone,
Today and every day.
Let's take the time
To show them we care.
Let's take the time
To share our lives with them.
Let's take the time to talk!

Moments in the Sun

Do not cast your shadow
On someone else's
Moment in the sun.
For it may be
Their one and only time
Out of the shadows of life.

Allow them to enjoy it,
To bask in it,
To relax,
To relish the moment.
To let the sunlight
Warm their soul.

Be patient.
Wait for it.
Your time will come
As it does for each of us.
The time when you can
Enjoy your own
Moment in the sun.

No matter how dark
Your day may seem.
No matter how gloomy
The shadows may appear.
No matter how negative
You may feel.
The time will always come
For you to enjoy
Your moment in the sun.

Dare to be Different

In this world of sameness,
When people tell you
It can not be done
Be yourself, do it anyway
And dare to be different.

When life attempts to hold you back
Move away from the path of normalcy
Forging a new one for yourself
Challenge the roadblocks,
Overcome the obstacles
And dare to be different.

When others choose to deceive,
Be honest.
When others stop and surrender,
Continue on, never giving up.
When others cheat,
Play by the rules.
Always dare to be different.

When others say no,
Say yes.
When others see black and white,
See a bright and beautiful rainbow.
When others take the low road,
Take the high road.
Create your own course
And dare to be different.
Do not be afraid,

Never stop believing
In what you can accomplish.
Keep moving forward
And dare to be different.

Who we love,
What we believe,
How we choose
To live our lives,
Always remember,
Dare to be different.

We were never meant
To be the same
As everyone else.
Be proud of who you are
And always dare to be different.

Dare to Dream

We all need to dare to dream.
During the turbulent times in our
  lives.
When we are feeling isolated,
Dreams give us hope.
When we feel worn out and tired,
They give us the strength to carry on.

When we are ready to give up,
They motivate us into action.
When we think we have reached the
  end,
They inspire us to fight on.
When we are lonely and afraid,
They uplift our spirits.

Dreams are the keys
To unlocking a greater future.
They are the foundation
Upon which to build our destiny.
They are the motivation
To uncover new paths to follow.
They are the dazzling sunshine
At the end of each storm.

They offer us peace and tranquility
During the challenging journey ahead.
They help us to overcome
The roadblocks and barriers in our
  path.
They give us the energy
To persevere against all odds.

Throughout our lives,
Dreams will become the spark of
  inspiration.
They will light the flames of
  imagination.
They will unlock the doors of
  innovation.
If only we will dare to dream,
A bright and beautiful future awaits
  us!